Creole Gigi's
Cajun Kitchen

Cook with Love,

♡Gigi

We're all the same; just on different paths & journeys

~Gigi

Foreword:

's difficult to say where the divide falls - if a divide even exists - between "Cajun food" and "Creole food." hey are in so many ways identical, and any variations that exist might as well be attributed to geography s to ethnicity. For example, it may be that both Cajuns and Creoles in a certain community tend to make neir gumbo one way, while those in a certain community ten, twenty, or fifty miles away tend to make their umbo another way. Some may make their roux with flour and vegetable oil; others, with flour and butter, r flour and lard. Those living near water, whether a bayou or lake or the Gulf of Mexico, might rely more eavily for their fare on seafood; those living farther inland, in land-locked areas, might rely more heavily n beef, pork, and fowl. And there are many other possible regional variations.

umbo, in fact, serves to illustrate the several influences that came to bear on the origin and development f both Cajun and Creole food, and on the Cajun and Creole people themselves. These influences cluded French, Spanish, Native-American, and Afro-Caribbean sources. Cajuns and Creoles, for xample, borrowed the word "gumbo" from a West African term meaning "okra," a vegetable introduced to outh Louisiana by African slaves and used by many as an essential gumbo ingredient. They obtained filé owdered leaves of the sassafras tree) from Native Americans, using it to thicken and season gumbo. hey gave gumbo its spicy flavor by adopting red peppers, such as cayenne, from the Spanish and, timately, from the indigenous peoples of the Caribbean and Latin America. And the roux came from their rench heritage in continental Europe. (It's interesting to note that the earliest known reference to gumbo Louisiana dates to 1764 — fairly early in the colony's history.)

igi has gathered in this cookbook a number of Cajun and Creole recipes for your consideration. From a ulinary perspective, it probably matters less if the recipes are "Cajun" or "Creole" (or both) than how good e resulting dishes taste. And that's really the point of a good cookbook: to provide a compendium of elicious-sounding recipes that make delicious-tasting cuisine.

hane K. Bernard

hane K. Bernard is a writer, historian, and curator who lives in New Iberia, Louisiana. le is the author of several books about south Louisiana history and culture.

Introduction:

I grew up in the middle of sugarcane fields in Southwest Louisiana, in an area aptly known as "Grand Bois," meaning "Big Woods" in French. Grand Bois sits in the middle of Cajun Country. Along and near the interstate that connects Florida to California, the cities of Breaux Bridge, Parks, Henderson, Lafayette, St. Martinville, and New Iberia taught me about the importance of food in my culture. My childhood, though, is forever rooted in Grand Bois and those sugarcane fields. Our neighbor on the other side of the sugar fields was Mr. Bijou. Mr. Bijou didn't speak English, but my Mom would visit him every so often to chat with him in Cajun/Creole French.

These were Mr. Bijou's fields, and just as the cane was ripe, he was happy to let us reach under our barbwire fence and grab our own personal bounties of sweet, ripe cane. As soon as you were old enough to handle a pocketknife (at a far less tender age than nowadays), you got to cut your very own stalk of cane. The joy of stripping that cane's outer shell and the getting the first chew of the season was a magical delight - eyes wide open as a rush of pure heaven hit your tongue. Sucking into all that wonderful sweetness remains one of the best, yet simplest, memories of my childhood.

Lazy summer days were filled with humidity and hanging upside down in my favorite front yard tree. When I wasn't pestering my big sister, Monique, I always found an adventure outside. Lemonade stands, which didn't require a permit, were always an exciting time. I was a skinny little Creole girl flagging down fast passing cars and trucks to stop and get a taste of my over-sugared homemade lemonade. Summer after summer in those hot Louisiana days, my adventures grew as I did. Those summers seemed endless - watching trail rides go by; running around kicking over crawfish mounds; chasing butterflies by day and chasing bright zigzagging fireflies by hot, humid night. Living on two acres with sparse country neighbors, getting visitors a.k.a. "company" was a big thing. Whether my neighbor's older son was down for a visit, or relatives ventured out to Grand Bois, it was like awaiting Santa Claus.

My neighbor across the busy country highway was like a second Mom to me. She was a true Cajun in every way. Mrs. Rose opened her home to us with no heads up necessary. Her husband, Mr. Paul, was an Italian from New York who like my Father (also from New York) fell in love with the quiet breeze of the hot and humid Louisiana country air. Many summers were spent in their backyard pond with their youngest child; canoeing through the trees, ducking low-hanging moss while fishing and picking at minnows with little sticks.

As I grew older, adventures allowed for beyond Mr. Bijou's sugarcane fields and Mrs. Rose and Mr. Paul's pond. Way past our mis-measured property lines laid old train tracks, wild blackberry bushes ripe for picking, and a broken wooden bridge over a long-ago dried-up creek. But, of all those lazy summer days, Sundays were the most eventful. We would go to Sunday school, church, and then home to get ready to either go to visit with or welcome family. My Mom was the youngest of ten children. Her Mom, Justine Noel Williams, born in 1898, would split her time living with us and my Aunt Mabel. She outlived my Father by a few years, who passed away from a sudden heart attack when I was 5 years old. This increased our family Sunday visits; trying to find solace amongst our many family members.

My Aunt Helen and Uncle Normie ventured out to Grand Bois more than anyone else after my Father passed away. Uncle Normie always had a beautiful, perfectly ripe watermelon for me. This is one of the few things that I overate growing up. My appetite consisted of wanting candy, candy, and more candy from the little country store with the gravel driveway and lot in between Grand Bois and the closest official "town/village" of Parks. I was the skinniest little niece that refused all the real food. Oh, if I could go back to those days now. I'll always regret the wonderful food of my Aunties, Uncles, and cousins that I passed up in my clueless young age. The smells of the Cajun trinity - onion, bell pepper, and celery - sautéing in those big black cast iron or shiny metal pots. The smell of roux melting down, ready to receive a bountiful portion of meats, poultry, or seafood to be cooked down for hours, filled their houses. The surprise and delight of what someone was cooking could be felt in the air. Oh, if I could go back and really know what I was passing up. Too full of cheap candy bars and too eager to see which cousins were playing in the "back rooms," I can only imagine what tastes I missed.

As I grew even older, though, I began to give in to those enchanting smells. And before my Mom was left as the last living child, I sampled and memorized those amazing, wonderful flavors of our Creole and Cajun past. For although I am ethnically Creole by majority, the Cajun food influences of my past reign supreme. From Uncle Chester's tripe or turtle stew when I spent time with his family – him, Aunt Stella and their three daughters - to my many cousins' houses; it's impossible to escape Cajun food in Southwest Louisiana.

I left Louisiana after high school. Through my journeys, I began to miss the unique food that I took for granted so much during my childhood. I would find a "Cajun" place on occasion throughout the US that never would, or even could, satisfy any speck of what Cajun food should look or taste like.

So, phone call by phone call, my Mom would guide me through some of the ingredients that were in my beloved favorites. Now, if you're from Louisiana, you'll understand why I had to make detailed phone calls. You'll be hard pressed to find solid old recipes with actual directions and measurements in Cajun Country. In Louisiana, people just cook. A little here, a little there and it's done when you're finished drinking "x" amount of beers. Alas, after years of trial and error, I found myself, too, following in those footsteps.

As my cooking became more for pleasure than necessity, I began cooking large amounts of meals. I started bringing them to meal groups to assist when friends were sick or had a loss in their family. Then, I would pack what didn't fit in our freezer and bring it to carline in containers. I would hand them out to my Mom friends and school staff at my kid's little Christian school in TX. I donated Cajun goodies, like my Gateau (Syrup cake), pralines, or bread pudding. They were always a hit! Slowly but surely, I started getting asked for recipes. Recipes!! Oh no! I didn't know what I did or how much I put of anything. I'm a Creole girl from Cajun Country - I just cook! One of the first times I tried to write a recipe for someone to make for a competition, I totally bombed! At that point, my food was always spot on, but I never stopped to measure anything; and that was my downfall. The crawfish étouffée recipe that I wrote ended up as a crawfish pontchartrain overflowing with much too much heavy cream. I was beyond embarrassed that I couldn't help friends re-create what I'd cooked dozens of times before that. So, my days of giving out "my recipes" were over after one time.

Occasionally, I'd try to remember to stop and write down ingredients, measurements, cooking times, etc. I'd quickly give up due to time constraints. So, there I was - a woman with a love for cooking only able to share my food if I cooked it myself. All the tweaking and perfection was left only for me to enjoy cooking.

However; now, after 7 years, I've found myself with once again the passion to finish what I started all those years ago. With my kids now teenagers, my 3rd career at a slow pace, and a drastic change with a close family member, I sat to think what I really wanted for my life. What really makes me happy and full? What calms me and stretches my heart to capacity, outside of my family? Alas, I've rediscovered my passion and determination over the last few years to put pen to paper and write some of my all-time Cajun meal hits. The wonderful thing about Cajun country is that everyone has their own way of making these dishes. However, they all end up being recognizable versions of the intended meal. With encouragement from family and friends, I've taken my versions and written them out for all to re-create. I am beyond thrilled to share my love of true Cajun food with everyone.

Mangeons! Let's eat!
Cook with Love & have lots of fun!

Laissez Les Bon Temps Ruler!

First and foremost -
Thank you to my own family for your patience while I completed this adventure

Thank you to Docq & Cheryl Gaspard (CDG Images), Danielle Guidry (Main Focus LLC), Cheri Lynn Soileau (Photography), Meagan Andrepont (Photography) , and Kerri Griechen (My Eye Photos) for capturing my vision. Additional thank you to LARC - Acadian Village (www.acadianvillage.org), Café Sydnie Mae (cafesydniemae.com), Le'Round Up Cajun Market, LA State Representative Mike Huval, Olde Tyme Grocery (www.oldetymegrocery.com), Daniela Barrantes, and Historian & Author Shane Bernard.   Special thank you Erik Jay Photography, Erik & Beth Jay, and portrait photographer, Tom Bertolotti.

Thank you to my recipe cooking testers – Monica Borel, Bridget Buck, Melanie Cole, Kimya Cruz, Jonathan Ellis, Linda Froelich, Aimee LeGrand, Susan Peters, Anika Porter, and Bonnie Wang. I'm happy that your families enjoyed you cooking with my recipes.

Front cover food photos courtesy Erik Jay Photography. Portrait photo above courtesy Tom Bertolotti in collaboration with Erik Jay Photography.

Thank you to all my family and friends for the encouragement & love

 Follow @__creolegigiscajunkitchen__ on social media

 for updates, photos, videos, cooking tips & more.

Instagram

6

Ode to Breaux Bridge ~ Laissez Les Bon Temps Ruler!

Breaux Bridge was listed as the "Prettiest Town in Louisiana" by _Architectural Digest_ in 2018

Above and far right: Breaux Bridge a.k.a. "Pont Breaux" bridge, built in 1950; replacing multiple bridges built since 1799
Photos courtesy: Left: Kerry Griechen; Middle and right: CDG Images

Public park, Breaux Bridge, LA
Photo courtesy: CDG Images

My Mother, Breaux Bridge, LA
(secondary) Centennial Parade, 1959

Public park, Breaux Bridge, LA
Photo courtesy: CDG Images

Downtown Breaux Bridge, LA
Photo courtesy: CDG Images

One of the award-winning restaurants in town
Photo courtesy: Main Focus LLC

Downtown Breaux Bridge, LA
Photo courtesy: Main Focus LLC

From left: A stroll across town; Le' Round Up Cajun Market balcony; Detailed architecture and beautiful grounds can be seen around Breaux Bridge Photos courtesy: CDG Images

Ode to Breaux Bridge ~ Laissez Les Bon Temps Ruler!

Round Up Cajun Flea Market

Downtown Breaux Bridge is lined with quaint old buildings housing restaurants, antique stores, local shops, and more…all along the glorious Bayou Teche Photos courtesy: CDG Images

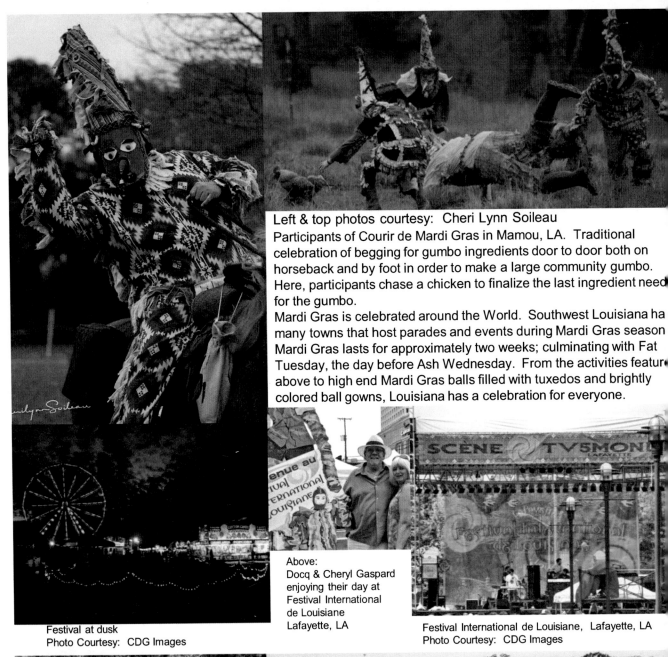

Left & top photos courtesy: Cheri Lynn Soileau
Participants of Courir de Mardi Gras in Mamou, LA. Traditional celebration of begging for gumbo ingredients door to door both on horseback and by foot in order to make a large community gumbo. Here, participants chase a chicken to finalize the last ingredient need for the gumbo.

Mardi Gras is celebrated around the World. Southwest Louisiana ha many towns that host parades and events during Mardi Gras season Mardi Gras lasts for approximately two weeks; culminating with Fat Tuesday, the day before Ash Wednesday. From the activities featur above to high end Mardi Gras balls filled with tuxedos and brightly colored ball gowns, Louisiana has a celebration for everyone.

Above:
Docq & Cheryl Gaspard enjoying their day at Festival International de Louisiane
Lafayette, LA

Festival at dusk
Photo Courtesy: CDG Images

Festival International de Louisiane, Lafayette, LA
Photo Courtesy: CDG Images

Photo courtesy: Main Focus, LLC

Big black pot simmering for competition at the annual Rice & Gravy Festival,

Aerial view of Breaux Bridge Crawfish Festival Parc Hardy festivities
Photo courtesy: Main Focus, LLC

Breaux Bridge, LA

LA Wildlife: From left: Roseate Spoonbill; Red winged Blackbird; Egrets in a crawfish pond. Photos: Cheri Lynn Soileau

From left: Great Blue Heron; Alligator in a swamp; Louisiana State bird, Brown Pelican Photos courtesy: Cheri Lynn Soileau

Shrimp boat with an oil rig in The Gulf of Mexico. Fishermen and offshore oil workers have been an important
fabric of Louisiana's workforce. Photo Courtesy: Cheri Lynn Soileau

Farming is also an integral part of Southwest Louisiana. Above left: Tractors on a farm and hauling sugarcane
to a sugar mill. Right: Sugarcane tractor hauling harvested sugarcane to mill for processing.

10

Moss hanging from trees in Louisiana lake Photo courtesy: Cheri Lynn Soileau

Gorgeous, old Live Oak trees on
Avery Island, the home of Tabasco®

Old canoe in a swamp
Photo courtesy: Kerry Griechen

Jungle Gardens,® Avery Island, LA

Avery Island

Housing for Buddha Statue on Avery Island

Louisiana roots Photo courtesy: Kerry Griech

Table of Contents:

Alligator sunbathing under Cypress trees in Lake Martin, LA
This photo, front cover bayou photo, and back cover courtesy: Main Focus LLC

Notes and preferences before you start:

Cajun Power Garlic Sauce®	Brand of sauce made in Louisiana. An alternative is a mix of Tabasco® and garlic powder.
Creole Seasoning	My absolute preference is Tony Chachere's Creole Seasoning® There is also a low-salt version. A no salt alternative would be a mix of black pepper, cayenne, onion powder, garlic powder & chili powder
Diced	Dice no larger than the square to the right:
Jack Miller's Bar-b-que Sauce®	Brand of unique barbeque sauce made in Louisiana. There isn't really an easy alternative. You may cook down onions, bell pepper, and celery until tender and add to a mild, tomato or mustard based barbecue sauce.
Kitchen Bouquet Browning & Seasoning Sauce®	I use this sauce in some of my smothered dishes. It has a unique seasoning flavor and helps with browning meat.
Roux	A cooked down mixture of flour and oil. Recipes for both a large or a single batch of roux are included in the cookbook. Alternatively or until you have mastered making a roux, I suggest the brand of Ragin Cajun Dark Roux®
Season liberally	Use enough seasoning to cover all parts of food thoroughly.
Tabasco®	Preferred. Alternatives would be a Louisiana (only) brand hot sauce

If you are a fan of <u>very</u> spicy dishes, feel free to add more Creole seasoning, cayenne, or hot sauce to your dish <u>at the end</u>. Otherwise, these recipes are suited for everyone's palates; written with the perfect amount of "kick" – respecting Cajun tradition, but not overwhelmingly spicy. All prep and cooking times are approximate. Most Cajun and Creole food taste amazing because it has been cooked slowly and seasoned well. This is one of the main reasons for the wonderful flavors of the multi-culturally infused food from Louisiana.

Detailed recipes: Why all the precise detail and different cooking temperatures? In Louisiana, we don't measure our ingredients, cooking times, or use a recipe guide. Our food is passed on by relatives and tweaked according to the cook's preferences. This is done by watching, helping, or being given a list of "most" of the ingredients with no directions or recipes. I've taken the time to note every step of my cooking process. This will aid you in re-creating my exact meals, so use every ingredient (unless listed as optional) and change temperatures as listed or as needed. All cooking appliances do not heat or maintain the same amount of heat, so pay attention to your dishes while cooking. Your taste buds will thank you!

Please note that I do not have <u>any</u> affiliations or interests in any brands mentioned. These are the brands that I personally purchase and use. Products mentioned may be purchased online.

Appetizers:

Great Blue Heron flying over Lake Martin, LA
Photo courtesy: Main Focus LLC

CREOLE GIGI'S
CAJUN KITCHEN

Today's Special

Appetizers for Dinner

Bacon Deviled Eggs

Crawfish Spinach Dip

Mini Crawfish Pies

Andouille Gouda Bit

A
L
W
A
Y
S

O
P
E
N

Crawfish Spinach Dip

2 packages frozen spinach

1 lb crawfish tails, defrosted

1/3 cup aged white cheddar

1/3 cup smoked Gouda, cut into small squares

1 cup sharp cheddar, cut into small squares

3 slices American cheese

1/4 cup heavy whipping cream

2 tsp butter

1 tsp minced garlic

1/8 cup diced onion

1 tbsp Creole seasoning

Cheesecloth or lint-free paper towels

Servings: 8-10

Prep Time: 10 minutes
Cook Time: 45 minutes

Preheat oven to 350.

Put frozen spinach in large, microwaveable dish. Microwave on high for 5 minutes; stir; continue microwaving for 2 minutes. Remove from microwave and strain remaining water from spinach using cheesecloth (or paper towels pressing the spinach in the dish to remove excess water). Add Creole seasoning, cheese, heavy cream, garlic, onions, and butter. Mix well. Bake for 25 minutes, stirring after 15 minutes. Stir in crawfish tails and bake for additional 10 minutes.

Serve with Tortilla or Pita chips

Mini Crawfish Pot Pies

1 dozen mini pie shells or 2 whole pie crusts - defrosted

Mini muffin pan lightly sprayed with nonstick spray

1 lb crawfish tails

1/2 cup heavy cream

1/4 cup minced garlic

1/2 cup diced onions

1/4 cup green bell pepper, diced

1 stalk celery, diced

1/4 cup chopped parsley

1/2 tsp green onions, sliced

2 tbsp butter

1 tbsp melted butter

1 tbsp Ragin Cajun Dark Roux® OR my homemade roux

3 tbsp cornstarch

2 tsp Creole seasoning

¼ tsp cayenne pepper

1 cup water

Servings:
Approximately 1 dozen

Prep Time: 10 minutes
Inactive: 10 minutes
Cook Time: 25 minutes

Prepare and preheat mini pie shells according to package directions for filling pies. If using whole pie crusts, cut pie crusts with round cookie cutter into 4-inch diameters. Take cut-outs and mold them gently into muffin pan. Using a sharp knife, mark a small "x" through the bottom of each crust. Bake in 350 oven for 5-6 minutes, until firm. Remove from oven. Baste with melted butter. Set aside.

Melt butter over medium-high heat in large sauté pan. Add onion, bell pepper, and celery to pan. Sauté for 5 minutes. Lower heat to medium. Add roux and cornstarch; melt into veggies. Add water and stir until blended. Add heavy cream and stir for 5 minutes. Add Creole seasoning, cayenne, ¼ cup parsley, green onions, minced garlic, and crawfish tails. Cook for 3 minutes. Remove from heat. Let mixture cool for 10 minutes. Preheat oven to 350 while mixture is cooling. Spoon mixture into pie shells. Bake in preheated oven for 10 minutes. Cool for 10-15 minutes before serving. Garnish with extra parsley, if desired.

Easy Crawfish Bread Bites

lbs crawfish tails

large "day-old" French bread, cut in half lengthwise

tbsp butter, cut up for easier melting

tbsp cornstarch

cup + 1 ½ tsp heavy whipping cream

/4 cup water

/4 cup diced onions

/4 cup diced bell pepper

stalks green onion, diced

tbsp minced garlic

tbsp Creole seasoning

tsp black pepper

/2 tsp red chili flakes

cups shredded cheddar cheese

slices provolone cheese

Servings: 10-12

Prep Time: 10 minutes
Cook Time: 50 minutes

reheat oven to 400.

dd butter to medium sauté pan or pot over medium-high heat. After butter has melted, add onions nd bell pepper to pot. Sauté for 3-4 minutes. Add cornstarch and water. Quickly lower temperature low-medium and stir. Add Creole seasoning, garlic, and 1 cup heavy cream to pan. Raise mperature to medium heat. Stirring constantly; continue cooking for 10 minutes, until base has ickened. Turn stove burner off. Season crawfish tails with black pepper and red chili flakes; then dd to pan. Cook for 3 minutes over low-medium heat. Remove pan from heat and allow to cool for 2- minutes. Stir in 1 ½ tsp cold or room temperature heavy cream (keeps mixture from overheating nd clumping). Place sliced French bread on baking sheet and slowly spoon crawfish mixture over rench bread slices. Do not overfill bread. Immediately place in oven. Bake for 10 minutes on center ven rack. Sprinkle green onions evenly over slices of French bread. Place slices of provolone heese on crawfish then evenly sprinkle cheddar cheese. Continue baking for 5 additional minutes. ut oven on high broil (do NOT move rack up). Do NOT walk away from oven. Carefully watching read in oven, broil for 2-3 minutes. Remove from oven. Allow to cool for 10 minutes before serving. ut into slices for serving.

Seafood Quiche

1 large deep-dish pie crust

4 large eggs

1 lb crawfish tails

1/2 lb peeled & deveined shrimp tails, chopped

1/2 cup lump crabmeat

1/2 cup heavy whipping cream

1/4 cup green onions

1/4 cup diced onion

1/4 cup minced garlic

1 tbsp butter

1 tbsp Creole seasoning

1/4 tsp red chili pepper flakes

Servings: 8-10

Prep Time: 10 minutes
Cook Time: 40 minutes

Preheat oven to 350.

Bake pie crust in preheated oven for 3- 5 minutes or until slightly browned. Remove from oven.

Melt butter over medium heat in small sauté pan. Add onion and sauté. In a large bowl, add eggs, heavy whipping cream, seafood, green onions, garlic, Creole seasoning, red pepper, and cooled, sautéed onions. Mix well. Slowly pour mixture into pie crust. Bake in preheated oven for 25-30 minutes. Cool 10 - 15 minutes before serving.

Crab Mac & Cheese Bites

3 Cups Elbow macaroni

8 oz real crabmeat (jumbo or lump)

2 tbsp butter

4 tbsp butter

2/3 cup half and half

2 cups shredded sharp cheddar

4 oz white cheddar

6 slices American cheese

2 tbsp flour

1 egg yolk (only)

1/2 tsp Black pepper

1/2 tsp White pepper

1/4 tsp Tabasco®

2 tsp red chili flakes

1/4 cup flour seasoned with 1 tsp Creole seasoning

Breading mix:

1/4 cup flour

1 cup plain breadcrumbs

Creole seasoning

2 eggs, beaten

Parsley for garnish

Dip: Mix together

1 cup mayo

¾ cup ketchup

1 tsp Cajun Power Garlic Sauce® or Tabasco®

Servings: approx. 36 balls

Prep Time: 30 minutes
Inactive: 1 hour
Cook Time: 40 minutes

Bring 6 cups water to a boil in large pot on stove. Stir in elbow macaroni and boil according to the time listed on package. Remove from heat and drain in colander. In pot, melt 4 tbsp butter over medium heat. Add 1 tbsp flour and stir until smooth. Remove from heat. Add half and half, cheeses, black & white pepper, and Tabasco® into the pot. Replace pot on burner over medium heat and stir until blended. Turn off burner. Season 'ready to eat' crabmeat with ½ tsp Creole seasoning. Add macaroni, egg yolk, 2 tbsp butter, red chili flakes, and crabmeat to pot; blend evenly with cheese sauce. Take ¼ cup seasoned flour and sprinkle evenly over coated macaroni. Using hands, begin firmly forming balls of macaroni and place into mini muffin pan or into freezer safe container.   Put dish/pan of macaroni balls in freezer for 1 hour. Fill a medium heavy-bottomed pot with at least one-inch vegetable oil on stove over medium heat. Remove balls from freezer and use a tablespoon to gently loosen from pan. Separately put flour, breadcrumbs, and beaten eggs in 3 separate bowls. Sprinkle ¼ tsp Creole seasoning on eggs, 2 tsp on breadcrumbs, and 1 tsp on flour. One by one, roll macaroni ball in flour, then egg, then breadcrumbs; repeat dip into egg and then breadcrumbs. Place on platter as you go until ready to fry all balls. You'll get a fast rhythm going, so it won't take that long. Take a pinch of flour and throw it in the pot to see if it sizzles. If it does, your oil is ready for the balls. Drop balls, being careful not to crowd pot or pan; turning until golden brown, about 6-7 minutes. Transfer balls to a paper towel lined plate to drain oil. Sprinkle with parsley flakes and serve with dip as soon as possible.

Andouille & Gouda Cheese Bites

4 links andouille sausage, casing removed, and sausage crumbled

1 cup breadcrumbs

2/3 cup half and half

4-6 oz smoked gouda cheese, cut into small squares or sliced

1 egg yolk

6 slices pickled jalapenos (from jar), diced

Breading mix:

1/4 cup flour

Flour for dusting

1 cup plain breadcrumbs

Creole seasoning for sprinkling

2 eggs, beaten

Dip: Mix together

1/3 cup mayonnaise

1/4 cup ketchup

6 tbsp yellow mustard

1/8 tbsp Cajun Power Garlic Sauce® (or Tabasco® and a couple of pinches of garlic powder)

Servings: 8-10

Prep Time: 10 minutes
Inactive: 1 hour
Cook Time: 30 minutes

Either slice or peel casing off andouille and crumble by hand. Put crumbled sausage in large mixing bowl. Add breadcrumbs, gouda, jalapeno, and egg yolk. Mix well with hands until uniformly together. Roll into balls and place in dish.   Put dish of balls in freezer for 30 minutes to 1 hour.

Remove balls from freezer. Fill a medium heavy-bottomed pot to 1/3 with vegetable oil on stove over medium heat. Separately put flour, breadcrumbs, and beaten eggs in 3 separate bowls. Sprinkle ½ tsp Creole seasoning on all three ingredients, adding ½ tsp more to flour. One by one, roll ball in flour, then egg, then breadcrumbs; repeat dip into egg and then breadcrumbs. Take a pinch of flour and throw it in the pot to see if it sizzles. If it does, your oil is ready for the balls. Drop balls, no more than 6 at a time; turning until golden brown. Transfer balls to a paper towel lined plate to drain oil. Serve within 5 minutes with dip.

Bacon Deviled Eggs

Party, party, party. What would Louisiana be without food and celebrations amongst family and friends? Whether it be a potluck, holiday, christening, wedding, or one of the over 400 festivals hosted annually in Louisiana, you can bet that many home cooked foods will be there. When you're bringing any food to a potluck, you may want something simple and quick to make. These deviled eggs are something familiar to everyone, with a simple twist.

Servings: 1 dozen

Prep Time: 5 minutes
Inactive: 15 minutes
Cook Time: 15 minutes

6 large eggs

3-4 strips applewood smoked bacon, cooked & crumbled

4 tbsp mayonnaise

2 tbsp yellow mustard

1/2 tsp Creole seasoning

Fresh or dried chives for garnish

Paprika

Boil, peel, and cut eggs in half. (Tip: after boiling eggs, rinse with cold water and add ice. This will make the shells come off more smoothly). Remove egg yolks. Set aside egg white halves. Mix egg yolks, mayonnaise, mustard, and Creole seasoning in small bowl until smooth. Put mixture into egg white shells. Cover & refrigerate for 15-20 minutes or until ready to serve. When ready to serve, sprinkle paprika, bacon pieces, and chives onto eggs. Serve immediately.

Blackberry BBQ Meatballs

1 lb lean ground beef

1 cup fresh blackberries

1/3 cup sugar

1 tsp butter

1 egg yolk

1 tsp flour

1 tsp parsley

1 slice white bread, crust removed

2 tsp Creole seasoning

Favorite BBQ sauce

Servings: approx. 20 meatballs

Prep Time: 15 minutes
Inactive: 1 hour, 10 minutes
Cook Time: 35 minutes

In a heavy pot over medium heat, melt butter. Add sugar and blackberries. Stir and mash blackberries while the sauce forms. Continue stirring for 5 minutes. Remove from heat and allow to cool for 10 minutes. Add ground beef to large mixing bowl and season with Creole seasoning. Add cooled blackberry mixture, flour, egg yolk, parsley, and bread slice to bowl and blend well into ground beef using hands. Form into 1 to 1 ½ inch diameter balls and refrigerate for 1 hour. Heat grill to medium-high / 350 degrees. Baste meatballs with BBQ Sauce. Place meatballs on pre-heated grill and cook for 12-15 minutes, turning halfway through, until browned. Serve warm.

Cajun Chicken Wings

2 dozen chicken wings or drumettes

1 cup flour for dusting

1 tbsp Creole seasoning + more

1 tsp white pepper

Buttermilk

Vegetable or peanut oil

Dip:

1 cup mayonnaise

¾ cup Ketchup

1 tsp Cajun Power Garlic Sauce® or Tabasco®

Servings: 2 dozen

Prep Time: 10 minutes
Inactive: 12 hours
Cook Time: 20 minutes

Season chicken with 1 tbsp Creole seasoning and 1 tsp white pepper. In a large mixing bowl, add seasoned chicken and liberally pour buttermilk over chicken until covered. Refrigerate overnight. In a large pot, add vegetable oil and heat over medium high heat. Remove chicken from refrigerator and let excess buttermilk drip off. Lightly dust chicken with flour seasoned with 2 tsp Creole seasoning. Add chicken in small batches and fry. Alternatively, skip flour and aircrisp in an aircrisper according to manufacturer directions. Drain chicken on paper towels. Serve warm.

For dip, mix dip ingredients together.

Soups:

Holiday Season =
GUMBO WEATHER!!

Christmas around Acadiana
Photo courtesy: Docq Gaspard

Christmas around Acadiana
Photo courtesy: Docq Gaspard

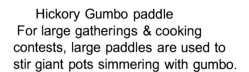

Hickory Gumbo paddle
For large gatherings & cooking
contests, large paddles are used to
stir giant pots simmering with gumbo.

25

Acadian Village at **Christmastime**
Lafayette, LA

Photos courtesy: CDG Images
Permission for use: LARC & Acadian Village
www.acadianvillage.org

Photo courtesy: Erik Jay Photography

One cardinal rule of being a Louisiana native has to do with the weather. On the first cold day of fall or winter, you can almost hear the clinking of big gumbo pots across the state. We call it "Gumbo Weather." This is an exciting time for everyone. The heat and humidity of the hot 100 + degree Louisiana summer ending is cause for celebration. Gumbo is Louisiana's comfort food. The joy of sampling a different version of everyone's gumbo is magical. Although tastes vary slightly, natives are almost always in agreement – NO TOMATOES OR CORN in our Cajun Gumbo! Although some Creole gumbo may include tomatoes for some in New Orleans' okra gumbo; I've noticed that Southwest Louisiana mostly sticks to a Cajun style gumbo. A roux, poultry, sausage, and/or seafood, along with the Cajun Trinity - onions, green bell pepper, and celery – are my area's basic gumbo ingredients. The wonderful, rich flavor of gumbo is gained by hours of integrating the unique taste of roux, seasonings, and proteins. I won't say any names, but a non-Louisiana native friend of mine tasted my gumbo for the first time. Her response upon her first taste was "I'm going to go home and bathe in this." That's one of the best compliments you could ever give a Louisiana cook. I hope that your gumbo get's the same praise! Take your time and enjoy a great bowl (or two) of Louisiana's comfort meal of choice.

Ca c'est bon! That's good!

Chicken & Sausage Gumbo

lbs boneless, skinless chicken breasts or tenders, cut into cubes
lbs trimmed boneless, skinless chicken thighs, cut into cubes
bone in chicken drumsticks
links smoked beef sausage
large white onion, diced
large green bell pepper, diced
stalk celery, diced
resh parsley sprigs for garnish
reole seasoning
2 tsp cayenne pepper
lack pepper
abasco®
whole bay leaves
) oz roux (1 ¼ jar of Ragin Cajun Roux®)
egetable oil
ooked rice, 1/2 cup per serving
all, large heavy bottomed **10 to 15 quart** stock pot (A Cajun favorite is the Magnalite® brand)

Servings: 10-15

Prep Time: 20 minutes
Cook Time: 4 hours, 45 minutes

eat 3 tbsp oil (use oil from roux jar if available) in large stock pot over high heat over largest stove burner available. dd diced onion, bell pepper, and celery and sauté for 8 minutes; stirring frequently. Lightly season with ½ tbsp reole seasoning. Lower temperature to medium-high heat. Add 3 cups water. Slowly add roux, stirring constantly to veggies and water. Roux must melt thoroughly into water as any chunks of roux may burn and ruin the gumbo. fter roux has melted (check the bottom of the pot for chunks of roux and break up with a large wooden spoon and blespoon), begin slowly adding water to stock pot, 3 cups at a time and stirring in between, until filled; leaving at ast 2 inches to the top to allow for boiling. <u>Additional</u> water should not exceed 12-15 cups. Add 2 tablespoons reole seasoning and ½ tsp cayenne pepper to pot. Raise temperature to high and bring to a boil, stirring constantly ntil roux has mixed with water. Melting the roux and bringing to a boil may take up to 20 minutes. Add chicken umsticks (only) to pot. Lower temperature to medium and keep on a low boil for 1 hour, stirring occasionally. Add ay leaves to pot, then remove after 2 minutes (they should be floating at the top); discard bay leaves. Do NOT leave ay leaves in under any circumstances, as they will overpower all flavors. Lightly season remaining chicken with 1 p black pepper and a few sprinkles of Creole seasoning. Add remaining chicken to gumbo stock pot. Skim and scard any excess oil (do not remove veggies) off the top of the gumbo. This may take up to 5 minutes; however, is necessary step for a better, non oily gumbo. Continue cooking for 3 hours, stirring occasionally, paying attention to e bottom of the pot. During the cooking process, raise heat to medium-high and boil for 3 minutes (don't boil over) d then lower back to medium heat, three to four times (about every hour). Cook sausage in skillet according to ckage directions. Drain on paper towels and cut into ½ inch slices. Add sausage to gumbo. Stir gumbo and add a sh of Tabasco® Remove and discard the drumstick skin and bones. Allow gumbo to rest for 15-20 minutes before rving. Serve over ½ cup cooked rice per serving. Garnish with fresh parsley. Allow gumbo to cool completely fore storing leftovers in refrigerator.

Chicken & Shrimp Gumbo

3 lbs boneless, skinless chicken breasts or tenders cut into cubes
3 lbs trimmed boneless, skinless chicken thighs cut into cubes
2 bone in chicken drumsticks
3 lbs medium raw shrimp, peeled and deveined
1 large white onion, diced
1 large green bell pepper, diced
1 stalk celery, diced
Fresh parsley sprigs for garnish
Creole seasoning
1/2 tsp cayenne pepper
Black pepper
2 whole bay leaves
20 oz homemade roux (or 1¼ jars of Ragin Cajun Roux®), loosened from container
Vegetable oil
Cooked rice, 1/2 cup per serving
Tall, large heavy bottomed **10 to 15 quart** stock pot (A Cajun favorite is the Magnalite® brand)

Servings: 10-15

Prep Time: 20 minutes
Cook Time: 4 hours, 45 minutes

Heat 3 tbsp oil (use oil from roux jar if available) in large stock pot over high heat over largest stove burner available. Add diced onion, bell pepper, and celery and sauté for 8 minutes; stirring frequently. Lightly season with ½ tbsp Creole seasoning. Lower temperature to medium-high heat. Add 3 cups water. Slowly add roux, stirring constantly into veggies and water. Roux must melt thoroughly into water as any chunks of roux may burn and ruin the gumbo. After roux has melted (check the bottom of the pot for chunks of roux and break up with a large wooden spoon and tablespoon), begin slowly adding water to stock pot, 3 cups at a time and stirring in between, until filled; leaving at least 2 inches to the top to allow for boiling. <u>Additional</u> water should not exceed 12-15 cups. Add 2 tablespoons Creole seasoning and ½ tsp cayenne pepper to pot. Raise temperature to high and bring to a boil, stirring constantly until roux has mixed with water. Melting the roux and bringing to a boil may take up to 20 minutes. Add chicken drumstick (only) to pot. Lower temperature to medium and keep on a low boil for 1 hour, stirring occasionally. Add bay leaves pot, then remove after 2 minutes (they should be floating at the top); discard bay leaves. Do NOT leave bay leaves in under any circumstances, as they will overpower all flavors. Lightly season remaining chicken with 1 tsp black pepper and a few sprinkles of Creole seasoning. Add remaining chicken to gumbo stock pot. Skim and discard any excess (do not remove veggies) off the top of the gumbo. This may take up to 5 minutes; however, is a necessary step for a better, non oily gumbo. Continue cooking for 3 hours, stirring occasionally, paying attention to the bottom of the pot. During the cooking process, raise heat to medium-high and boil for 3 minutes (don't boil over) and then lower back to medium heat, three to four times (about every hour). Season shrimp with 1 tsp black pepper and add to pot; stir. Continue cooking for 3 minutes. Remove and discard the drumstick skin and bones. Allow gumbo to rest for 15-20 minutes before serving. Serve over 1/2 cup cooked rice per serving. Garnish with fresh parsley. Allow gumbo to cool completely before storing leftovers in refrigerator.

Potato salad (recipe in "Sides" section - omit green olives when making for gumbo side) and French bread is a must as sides with gumbo. Hint: Gumbo also tastes better the next day.

Seafood Gumbo

5 lbs medium raw shrimp, peeled and deveined
1 blue (gumbo) crab per serving/person + a few extra
16 oz oysters, undrained; reserve oyster liquid for cooking
1 large white onion, diced
1 large green bell pepper, diced
1 stalk celery, diced
Fresh parsley sprigs for garnish
Creole seasoning
1/2 tsp cayenne pepper
Black pepper
Tabasco®
2 whole bay leaves
20 oz homemade roux (or 1¼ jars of Ragin Cajun Roux®), loosened from container
Vegetable oil
Cooked rice, 1/2 cup per serving
Tall, large heavy bottomed **10 to 15 quart** stock pot (A Cajun favorite is the Magnalite® brand)

Servings: 10-15

Prep Time: 10 minutes
Cook Time: 4 hours

Heat 3 tbsp oil in large stock pot over high heat. Add diced onion, bell pepper, and celery and sauté for 8 minutes; stirring frequently. Lightly season with ½ tbsp Creole seasoning. Lower temperature to medium-high heat. Add 3 cups water. Slowly add roux, stirring constantly into veggies and water. Roux must melt thoroughly into water as any chunks of roux may burn and ruin the gumbo. After roux has melted (check the bottom of the pot for chunks of roux and break up with a large wooden spoon and tablespoon), begin slowly adding water to stock pot until filled, leaving at least 2 inches to the top to allow for boiling. Add 2 tablespoons Creole seasoning to pot. Raise temperature to high and bring to a boil, stirring constantly until roux has mixed with water. This may take up to 20 minutes. Lower temperature to medium and keep on a low boil for 1 hour, stirring occasionally. Add bay leaves to pot, then remove after 2 minutes (they should be floating at the top); discard bay leaves. Continue cooking for 2 ½ hours, stirring occasionally. During the cooking process, raise heat to a boil for 2 minutes and then lower back to medium heat, (every thirty minutes). Add crabs to pot and continue cooking for 3 minutes. Add remaining seafood to pot, along with 1 tsp black pepper, and a dash of Tabasco® to pot and stir. Continue cooking for another 3 minutes. Allow gumbo to rest for 15-20 minutes before serving. Serve over 1/2 cup cooked rice per serving. Garnish with fresh parsley.

Allow gumbo to cool completely before storing leftovers in refrigerator.

Potato salad (recipe in "Sides" section – omit green olives when making for gumbo side) and warm French bread is a must as sides with gumbo.

Hint: Gumbo tastes even better the next day as leftovers.

Crab & Sweet Corn Chowder

12-16 oz lump crabmeat

10-12 oz bag frozen sweet corn

1 medium yellow onion, diced

1 large stalk celery, diced

5 small red potatoes, cut into 1 to 1 ½ inch cubes

3 cups chicken broth

1 cup cold water added TO 2 tbsp flour and 2 tbsp cornstarch; mixed and ready to use

4 tbsp butter

1/2 tbsp Creole seasoning

1/4 tsp cayenne pepper

1/4 tsp Black pepper

1 cup heavy whipping cream

3 tbsp bacon grease (preferred) or vegetable oil

Crumbled bacon from making bacon grease for topping (if desired)

Servings: 4-6

Prep Time: 15 minutes
Cook Time: 80 minutes

In a tall stock pot, heat 3 tbsp bacon grease or vegetable oil over medium-high heat. Add potatoes and cook for 10 minutes, stirring frequently. Add onion and celery and continue cooking for 10 minutes. Add butter and allow to melt. Add water mixture, chicken broth, Creole seasoning, cayenne, and black pepper to stock pot. Raise temperature to high and bring to a boil. Boil for 5 minutes. Lower temperature to low-medium heat and simmer for 30 minutes, stirring occasionally. Raise heat to medium. Add corn and heavy whipping cream and continue cooking for 10 minutes, stirring frequently. Season crabmeat with 1 tsp Creole seasoning and add to pot. Continue cooking for 6-8 minutes. Let rest for 10 minutes. Top with crumbled bacon, if desired. Lightly grind black pepper over dish and garnish with parsley.

Entrees:

Entrees:

SHRIMP PO'BOYS

JAMBALAYA

SHRIMP ÉTOUFFÉE

CRAWFISH ÉTOUFFÉE

SHRIMP ÉTOUFFÉE

Shutterstock

Crawfish Étouffée

Although I consider my home to be Grand Bois, my official hometown is Breaux Bridge, LA. Breaux Bridge is the Crawfish Capital of the World. It is considered the heart of Cajun Country. Founded in 1766, Breaux Bridge was one of the first settlements of the Acadians. Every first weekend of May, the city holds their annual Crawfish Festival. My cousin, referred to as Uncle Alvin and his late wife, Aunt Lulla, celebrated this time with huge crawfish boils at their house. Our family and friends still join Uncle Alvin and his family every year! Many other residents also have large lawn parties to celebrate the season. The entire city shuts down to celebrate the abundance of crawfish meals that are shared with family, friends, and visitors alike. Untold tons of crawfish are boiled and enjoyed, along with other amazing crawfish dishes. When I was younger, my family found excitement walking through the city and seeing license plates from around the US and Canada of people that came to enjoy our culture and food. Cajun and Zydeco music fill the air as kids enjoy the carnival and adults enjoy the party. Dancing, eating, drinking, and more are in abundance during this eagerly awaited weekend.

Servings: 4-6
Prep Time: 10 minutes
Cook Time: 50 minutes

1 lb Louisiana crawfish tails with fat
1/2 cup white onion, diced
1/2 cup green bell pepper, diced
1/2 stalk celery, diced
1 stalk green onion, cut into slices (for garnish)
4 tbsp tomato paste
1/2 cup flour
2 tbsp cornstarch
1 tbsp homemade roux or Ragin Cajun Dark Roux®
8 tbsp unsalted butter, cut into pieces for easier melting

1/2 cup heavy whipping cream
1 tbsp + 1 tsp Creole Seasoning
1/4 tsp paprika
1/4 tsp minced garlic
1/4 tsp black pepper
1/4 tsp cayenne pepper
Dash of Tabasco®
3 cups water

In a heavy-duty pot over medium-high heat, melt butter. Add diced white onion, bell pepper, and celery. Add 1 tbsp Creole seasoning. Sauté for 5 minutes. Lower heat to medium and stir in flour, cornstarch, and roux; mixing for 5 minutes. Add 3 cups water, heavy cream, tomato paste, garlic, cayenne, and paprika. Raise heat to high and bring to a boil, stirring occasionally, for 2-3 minutes. Lower heat to low. Cover and simmer for 30 minutes, stirring occasionally (every 10 minutes). Season crawfish tails with 1 tsp Creole seasoning. Uncover pot and raise heat to high and cook for 2 minutes. Lower heat to low-medium. Stir in ¼ tsp black pepper, Tabasco,® and crawfish tails. Cover, and cook for 5 minutes. Turn off stove burner, remove pot from burner, and let stand 10 minutes before serving.

Serve over rice and garnish sparsely with green onions.

Mom's Old-Fashioned Crawfish Bisque

1 small white onion, diced

1 small bell pepper, diced

1 stalk celery, diced

1/2 tsp minced garlic

1/2 stalk green onion, chopped

1/8 cup dried parsley

1/4 cup melted butter

3 tbsp melted butter

2, 1 tbsp butter

1/2 cup roux

1/2 cup heavy whipping cream

1/2 tsp Worcestershire sauce

2 tbsp tomato paste

1 cup plain breadcrumbs

1/4 cup plain breadcrumbs

1/4 cup flour

1 tsp cornstarch

Creole seasoning

1/4 tsp cayenne pepper

12 - 15 crawfish heads cleaned out (see below)

1/2 lb crawfish tails

1/2 lb chopped crawfish tails with fat/liquid from package

6 cups water

Servings: 6-8

Prep Time: 1 hour
Cook Time: 2 hours

Stuffed crawfish
heads in base:

Crawfish Bisque over rice:

Crawfish heads:

After a crawfish boil, retain some heads of the boiled crawfish. Store in refrigerator until use for this recipe for up to 3 days. Remove and discard all membranes from heads. Pull off claws and reserve for garnish. Put crawfish heads in colander and rinse out in cold water in sink. Allow to air dry.

Continued on next page…

Mom's Old-Fashioned Crawfish Bisque
...continued

Preheat oven to 350 degrees

Base:

In a heavy bottomed pot on stove, melt 1 tbsp butter on medium high heat. When heated, add onion, bell pepper, celery, and garlic. Sprinkle with 1 tsp Creole seasoning and sauté for 5 minutes. Lower heat to medium and add roux, cornstarch, heavy whipping cream, Worcestershire sauce, cayenne, and tomato paste; stir until melted. Add 4 cups of water - 2 cups at a time; stirring in between. Raise heat to high and bring to a boil, stirring occasionally. Mix well. Lower heat to medium. Keep at a low boil and continue cooking for 30 minutes, stirring occasionally. Stir in 1 tsp Creole seasoning. Stir well and cook for 5 minutes.

Remove from heat and set aside.

Stuffing:

In a mixing bowl add 1 cup breadcrumbs seasoned with Creole seasoning (about 3 tsp), chopped crawfish tails with fat, 3 tbsp melted butter, and parsley. Mix well. In a separate container, mix 1/4 cup breadcrumbs and 1/4 cup flour. Slightly dap crawfish heads with water, then coat each in breadcrumb/flour mixture. Stuff inside of crawfish heads with crawfish, fat, 3 tbsp butter, breadcrumb and parsley mixture.

Completion:

In a baking dish, add 1/4 cup melted butter. Place stuffed heads, stuffing side up, onto baking dish with melted butter. Bake in preheated oven for 30 minutes. Remove from oven.

Turn heat back on medium high heat for pot with base. Add 1/2 lb crawfish tails. Slowly add stuffed crawfish heads into pot with stuffing faced down. Lower temperature to low medium heat. Cook for 10 minutes. Remove from heat. Garnish with several crawfish claws and green onions. Serve over rice.

Shrimp Étouffée

2 lbs medium raw shrimp, peeled & deveined

2 ½ tbsp tomato paste

1/4 cup white onion, diced

1/4 cup green bell pepper, diced

1/4 cup celery, diced

1 tbsp butter

1/4 cup heavy whipping cream

1/2 tbsp + extra Creole Seasoning

1 tsp homemade roux or Ragin Cajun Dark Roux®

1/4 tsp paprika

1/4 tsp cayenne pepper

4 tbsp flour

2 tbsp cornstarch

Vegetable oil

Fresh parsley (for garnish)

1/4 tsp Tabasco®and 1/4 tsp Worcestershire sauce 3 cups water

Servings: 4-6

Prep Time: 10 minutes
Cook Time: 50 minutes

In a heavy-duty pot on medium-high heat, heat 2 tbsp vegetable oil. Add diced onion, bell pepper, and celery. Sprinkle lightly with 1 tsp Creole Seasoning. Sauté for 5 minutes. Lower heat to low-medium. Add 3 tbsp vegetable oil, roux, 2 tbsp cornstarch, and 4 tbsp flour to pot. Stir well for 1-2 minutes until well blended. Add ½ tbsp Creole seasoning, tomato paste, paprika, cayenne pepper, heavy cream, and Tabasco®/Worcestershire sauce; stir, then add 3 cups water. Blend well and raise heat to high to bring to a boil. Continue stirring constantly for 3 minutes while boiling. Stir, reduce heat to low, cover, and continue cooking for 30 minutes, stirring frequently. After simmering, raise heat to high and stir for 1 minute; then lower heat to low-medium heat. Season shrimp lightly with ½ tsp black pepper. Add shrimp and butter. Cover and continue cooking for 3 minutes. Stir and recover, allowing to thicken 5-10 minutes. If you'd like a spicier etouffee, you can more Tabasco® and/or Creole seasoning to your individual serving.
Serve over rice, garnish with parsley.

This sauce will thicken in the refrigerator. If reheating etouffee leftovers, add 1-2 tbsp water before reheating.

Fried Shrimp Po'boys

I can't mention po'boys without mentioning my all-time favorite po'boy (a.k.a. "poorboy") place, Olde Tyme Grocery, in Lafayette, LA. Olde Tyme Grocery is just on the border of the local university, ULL (formerly USL). Olde Tyme is a right of passage for any college student at ULL. This small, old white wooden building with red accents houses an ordering counter with locally made Cajun sweet pies and treats, a large display case, drink coolers, and snack shelves filled with Louisiana made potato chips. Behind the counter, college students work fast to take orders and get them to the back of house for hungry students, businessmen or women, and everyday folk to enjoy to go or in the small self seating area to the right. Soft, but hearty Louisiana made French bread gets slathered with mayo and topped with shredded lettuce, tomato, meat or seafood, then a zig-zag of ketchup. This isn't regular meat or seafood. This is roast beef, dripping with flavorful gravy, among other tender meat choices. This is plump, juicy shrimp, oysters, or catfish; freshly fried with just enough hot oil still clinging to the light, golden brown batter. Hungry yet? Fill up on the po'boy if you'd like; but leave a little room for the bonus in the back. What else could make you smile on a hot, humid day besides a soft as a cloud; cold as, well...ice, snoball? Right behind Olde Tyme Grocery, in a miniature matching building is Murph's Snoball Stand. From tiny tots to their Great, Great Grands, Murph's will put a glisten in your eyes and a smile on your face. While waiting your turn, the rainbow-colored signs and list of fascinating flavors and toppings brings excitement. I'd wait in line, exploring the possibilities of each section of the snoball running down my cup with a different color and flavor. Oh those flavors...peach, watermelon, strawberry, coconut, cotton candy...the list goes on. Alas, when it was my turn to step up to the long step running across the front of the stand, my loyal flavors always seemed to win out - half ice cream flavor and half wedding cake flavor. You read that right! My bright yellow ice cream flavor was like eating sweet vanilla ice cream made of a million falling snowflakes. The colorless wedding cake flavor was like the softest, fluffiest wedding cake and icing melting in your mouth. Yet, I digress. Po'boys...yes, po'boys. Let's get to it!

Olde Tyme Grocery, Lafayette, LA
Photo courtesy: Main Focus LLC; Permission for use: Olde Tyme Grocery

Continued on next page...

Fried Shrimp Po'boys

lbs raw medium shrimp, peeled & deveined

cup yellow cornmeal and 2 cups flour, mixed together

egg yolks, beaten and 1/3 cup whole milk, mixed together

allon sized food storage bag (Ziploc bag or store brand)

reole seasoning for sprinkling

lack pepper for sprinkling

egetable oil for frying

arge platter lined with stack of paper towels

rench bread, ready to cut to 6 inches (small) or 12 inches (large); to be cut before serving

ayonnaise

etchup

hredded lettuce

liced tomatoes

Servings: 4-6

Prep Time: 15 minutes
Cook Time: 10 minutes

ll fryer pot 1/3 with vegetable oil and heat over medium heat. Add cornmeal/flour mixture to storage bag, season erally with Creole seasoning (about 3-4 tbsp), seal, and shake thoroughly to blend. Add egg yolk/milk mixture to a ixing bowl and lightly season with Creole seasoning. Season shrimp lightly with black pepper. Starting with pproximately 1/4 of shrimp, dip shrimp into egg/milk mixture, then add to storage bag and shake thoroughly. ontinue process until all shrimp are coated. Sprinkle a pinch of cornmeal/flour mixture into oil of fryer pot. If oil zzles, carefully begin adding coated shrimp into pot in small batches; being careful not to overcrowd. Fry until golden own, 3-4 minutes. Remove fried shrimp onto platter of paper towels and allow oil to drain. Repeat with remaining rimp. Slightly warm French bread in 225 oven for 3 minutes. Cut into chosen lengths and slice in half, leaving top d bottom connected in the middle. Dress bottom half of bread with mayonnaise, lettuce, and tomatoes. Add fried rimp, then zig-zag ketchup over fried shrimp. Serve immediately.

Murph's Snoball Stand
Photo courtesy:
Main Focus LLC
Permission for use:
Olde Tyme Grocery

Roast Beef Po'boys w/ Gravy

3 lb eye of round roast

1 tsp Kitchen Bouquet Browning & Seasoning Sauce®

Creole seasoning

1/2 cup red wine, preferably a cabernet sauvignon

1 medium yellow onion, chopped

1 small green bell pepper

1 tsp diced garlic

1 tbsp vegetable oil

3/4 cup flour seasoned with Creole seasoning

1 tsp cornstarch

French bread, ready to cut to 6 inches (small) or 12 inches (large); to be cut just before serving

Provolone cheese (optional)

Mayonnaise

Shredded lettuce

Sliced tomatoes

Servings: 4-6

Prep Time: 10 minutes
Cook Time: 4-8 hours

Set large crock pot on either high (4 hours) or low (8 hours). In a large, heavy bottomed skillet or pan, heat 1 tbsp vegetable oil over high heat. Season roast liberally with Creole seasoning and 1 tsp Kitchen Bouquet.® Add roast to pan, browning on all sides. Transfer roast to crock pot. Add onions and bell pepper to oil drippings in pan and sauté over medium heat for 5 minutes. Pour red wine over veggies in pan. Pour all contents in pan over roast in crock pot. Allow roast to continue cooking. After roast is done, transfer onto a platter. Turn crockpot to high. In a glass or small dish, add 3/4 cup seasoned flour, cornstarch, and 2 tsp Creole seasoning; then add 1 cup cold water and blend until there are no lumps. Add mixture to crock pot and stir. Allow mixture to cook until gravy forms and thickens, up to 20 minutes. Pour some gravy over roast and separate roast into pieces if needed. It should be very tender at this point.

Slightly warm French bread in 225 oven for 3 minutes. Cut into chosen lengths and slice in half, leaving top and bottom connected in the middle. Dress bottom of bread with mayo, lettuce, and tomatoes, if desired. You may choose other condiments if desired; e.g., mustard, pickles or omit listed condiments as desired. Place roast with gravy on bottom bread slice. Top with provolone cheese, if desired.

Fried Seafood Platter
(Crawfish, Shrimp, Oysters, Catfish)

Henderson, Louisiana is a town next to where I grew up. At the edge of Henderson lies a levee built to protect the area from flooding from the Atchafalaya Basin. Henderson is an integral place for fresh-water fishing in Louisiana. A trip to Henderson was always a treat for 3 reasons. T-Sue's Bakery had wonderful selections of freshly baked French bread, Cajun goodies, and my favorite, pecan sandies with whipped chocolate in the center. The second reason we'd travel the windy country roads to Henderson was to get fresh seafood. We would go into a large warehouse, brimming with just caught seafood and hard-working Louisiana fishermen. Mom would pick what she wanted to cook over the next few days and they would rinse off her fresh selections right in front of us. Also in Henderson was our favorite seafood restaurant, Pat's Fisherman's Wharf. This restaurant was just on the other side of the levee with a great water deck to enjoy. While waiting for our table, we would walk on the deck and see who could spot the biggest alligator below us. Alligators seemingly as big and old as dinosaurs would glide under the deck, zig-zagging around cattails, swamp lilies, and cypress to the water's edge. Pat's was usually my birthday dinner choice. This normally food intolerant Creole girl couldn't wait to have their enormous seafood platter, brimming with catfish, shrimp, oysters, crawfish, and a stuffed crab, placed in front of me. Anytime I make a seafood platter, sweet memories of Pat's deck bring me back to my childhood.

Continued on next page…

Photo courtesy: Meagan Andrepont

Photo courtesy: Meagan Andrepont

Photo courtesy: Meagan Andrepont

Photo courtesy: Cheri Lynn Soileau

42

Fried Seafood Platter
(Crawfish, Shrimp, Oysters, Catfish)
...continued

2 lbs raw shrimp, peeled & deveined; tails on

2 lbs cleaned crawfish tails

1 lb catfish fillets

3 cups flour + extra for sprinkling

3 cups yellow cornmeal

3 eggs, beaten with 2 cups milk (egg mixture)

1 half fresh lemon

Yellow mustard

Vegetable or peanut oil

Creole seasoning for seasoning

Servings: 4-6

Prep Time: 20 minutes
Cook Time: 45 minutes

In a large food storage or paper bag, add 2 cups of flour, 1 cup cornmeal, and season liberally with Creole seasoning. Shake bag well to mix thoroughly. Heat oil in a heavy bottomed, large pot or fryer, filling 1/3 of pot, over medium heat. Be sure that oil does not begin to smoke while heating. If so, turn off burner and allow to cool for 10 -15 minutes. Season all seafood liberally with Creole seasoning. Sprinkle some flour on the shrimp and crawfish. Dip raw shrimp and uncooked crawfish tails into egg wash, then bag of flour/cornmeal mix. Let sit for 5 minutes for batter to set. Meanwhile, in a large food storage or paper bag, add 1 cup of flour, 2 cups of cornmeal, and season liberally with Creole seasoning. Coat catfish fillets lightly with yellow mustard on all sides, then egg mixture. Dip into cornmeal/flour mix and be sure to coat catfish thoroughly. Sprinkle a bit of flour in heated oil to check for readiness to fry. If oil sizzles, you are ready to fry. Again, oil should not produce smoke, as this shows that it is too hot. Use a large, slotted spoon to slowly add crawfish and shrimp to frying pot in batches. Fry for 3-4 minutes until golden brown, placing finished seafood on paper towel lined plate or platter. After frying shrimp and crawfish, begin frying catfish, being careful to do it in batches to avoid overcrowding. Fry for 7 minutes, per side. Drain on paper towel lined platter. Serve all seafood together after spritzing with lemon.

Fried Catfish topped w/ Crawfish Sauce

1-2 lb catfish fillets

Yellow mustard

2 cups yellow cornmeal

2 eggs, beaten with 1 cup milk (egg mixture)

1 cup flour and 2 cups yellow cornmeal, mixed and seasoned with Creole seasoning

Creole seasoning

Servings: 4-6

Prep Time: 10 minutes
Cook Time: 30 minutes

Crawfish sauce:

1 cup heavy whipping cream

1 ½ cup whole milk

1/2 lb cleaned crawfish tails

½ tsp cornstarch

3 tbsp flour

3 tbsp butter

1 tsp Creole seasoning

Parsley for garnish

In a pan, melt butter over medium- high heat. Add 3 tbsp flour and stir well. Continue stirring for 2 minutes, until smooth and blended well. Slowly stir in heavy whipping cream, cornstarch, milk, and Creole seasoning. Lower temperature to medium and stir until blended smooth with no lumps. Add crawfish tails and cook for 3-4 minutes. Turn stove burner off and let stand, stirring occasionally until ready to use.

In a large pan or pot, fill to 3 inches of vegetable oil and heat over medium heat. In a large food storage or paper bag, add 1 cup of flour, 2 cups of cornmeal, and season liberally with Creole seasoning. Coat catfish fillets lightly with yellow mustard on all sides, then egg mixture. Dip into cornmeal/flour mix and be sure to coat catfish thoroughly. Sprinkle a bit of flour in heated oil to check for readiness to fry. If oil sizzles, you are ready to fry. Note, oil should not produce smoke, as this shows that it is too hot. Begin frying catfish, being careful to do it in batches to avoid overcrowding. Fry for 6-7 minutes, per side. Drain on paper towels lined platter. Plate fried catfish and *pour crawfish sauce over catfish fillets. *If sauce has over-thickened, add a tablespoon of milk, reheat on medium, then pour over catfish. Garnish with parsley and serve immediately.

Blackened Catfish

4-6 catfish fillets

2 tbsp Creole seasoning

2 tsp paprika

1 cup melted butter

1 tbsp butter per fillet

Servings: 4-6

Prep Time: 10 minutes
Cook Time: 15 minutes

Heat a large cast iron skillet over high heat on stove. In a small mixing bowl, combine Creole seasoning and paprika. Pour melted butter over each filet, covering all sides. Sprinkle seasoning mixture on all sides of fillets. Press seasoning down onto fillets so that they are coated well. Place each fillet in heated skillet and drizzle each with one tablespoon of melted butter. The skillet **will** smoke. Cook 4-5 minutes per side. Place fillets on platter, spritzing lightly with lemon wedge, and serve immediately over rice.

Lobster & Shrimp Fried Rice

1 lb peeled/deveined raw shrimp

2, 4-6 oz lobster tails, cut in bite sized cubes

2 eggs

1/3 cup white onions, chopped

1/2 tsp scallions, diced

1/4 cup carrots, diced

1 tsp minced garlic

1/2 tsp sesame seeds

Garlic powder

Creole seasoning

Soy sauce

4 cups cooked white rice

1 ½ tbsp butter

Safflower oil

Servings: 6-8

Prep Time: 10 minutes
Cook Time: 20 minutes

Heat wok over medium-high heat.

Add 1 tbsp safflower oil to wok. Add onions and carrots; sauté for 5-6 minutes. Add 1/2 tsp safflower oil to wok, crack eggs and scramble in wok. Push onions and eggs to side of wok. Add 1 tbsp butter to wok. Add shrimp, lobster, minced garlic. Season lightly with Creole seasoning while stirring. When seafood is done (about 4 minutes), add cooked rice, remaining 1/2 tbsp butter and scallions. Mix together with items in wok. Add soy sauce along sides of wok (do not saturate on top) and continue stirring. Sprinkle garlic powder, black pepper and sesame seeds. Gather mixture in round mound and remove from heat. Let steam off for 5 minutes before serving.

You may add diced chicken to this recipe also. Add raw small diced chicken as the first item and cook thoroughly. This will enhance the flavor of the dish.

P.S. Lobster is not a food staple in Louisiana. Sometimes I just like to mix it up for family & friends.

Red Beans & Rice w/ Sausage

1 lb package Camilla® dry red kidney beans
1/2 package hambone shanks
1/2 package smoked pork necks
2 links smoked sausage
1 large white onion, diced
1 large green bell pepper, diced
2 stalks celery, diced
2 tsp minced garlic
1 tsp parsley
5 whole dried bay leaves (in spice section)
2 tsp Tabasco®
2 tsp Cajun Power Garlic Sauce®
1 tsp cayenne pepper
1/2 tsp salt
1/2 tsp black pepper
1/4 tsp garlic powder
3 tbsp Creole seasoning
2 tbsp vegetable oil x 2

Servings: 10-15

Prep Time: 10 minutes
Inactive: 8 hours
Cook Time: 5 hours

Sort and rinse beans. Cover in a large bowl and soak in water for 8 hours. (Or soak in water with unseasoned meat tenderizer for one hour). Rinse beans in a colander and set aside. Fill a large heavy bottomed pot 3/4 with water. Add beans, 2 tbsp vegetable oil, Cajun Power®, bay leaves, cayenne pepper and smoked neck bones over medium heat. Be sure all beans are covered in water; add water if necessary.

In a saucepan add 2 tbsp vegetable oil. Add hambones and brown on each side; do not drain. Set aside hambones onto separate dish.

Add vegetables and 1 tbsp Creole seasoning to saucepan with hambone drippings and sauté over medium heat until transparent (about 6-8 minutes).

Add hambone and sautéed vegetables to beans. Stir all remaining ingredients **except** sausage to pot and bring to a boil. Stir, cover, and reduce heat to low. Simmer for 4 to 4 1/2 hours stirring every 30 minutes. When stirring, raise heat to medium for 2 minutes, then lower back to low. Make sure that the bottom of the pot is stirred also; making sure beans have not stuck to the bottom. Be sure to check water level and add water if necessary (beans should always have at least one inch of liquid covering them). Remove cover and remove 1/2 cup beans. Smash beans with a heavy spoon and mix back into pot. Add Tabasco.® Cut sausage and cook in saucepan used for hambone. Add to beans and cook for 3 minutes. Remove all bay leaves from pot and discard. Serve over rice, garnish with parsley. Note: Be sure beans are always covered with liquid or they will burn. When stirring, be sure to stir the bottom of the pot to avoid any beans sticking and burning at the bottom.

Seafood Jambalaya

1 cup crawfish tails

1 lb raw shrimp, peeled & deveined

8 oz drained crabmeat

8 oz drained oysters

1 medium white onion, diced

1 stalk celery, diced

1 tbsp minced garlic

1 tbsp parsley

1 tsp green onion, diced

3/4 cup canned chopped tomatoes

2 tbsp vegetable oil

2 tbsp roux

1 tbsp Creole seasoning

1/4 tsp cayenne pepper

2 cups uncooked rice

4 cups water

Servings: 8-10

Prep Time: 10 minutes
Cook Time: 70 minutes

In a heavy-bottomed pot over medium heat, heat vegetable oil. Add white onion and celery & sauté for 5 minutes.   Add roux; blend quickly; then add 4 cups water, Creole seasonings, tomatoes, and garlic. Raise temperature to high and bring to a boil. Continue a low boil for 15 minutes, stirring occasionally. Add rice and then reduce heat to low, simmering for 30-35 minutes or until rice is cooked thoroughly. Rice should not be dry. The texture should be moist, but not wet. Add seafood to pot, blending well. Cook for 10 minutes being careful to stir the bottom of the pot occasionally. Add parsley and blend well into mixture. Pat down rice to make the top even and let sit for 5 minutes before serving.

Chicken & Sausage Jambalaya

2 lbs boneless *chicken breasts or tenders (easier to cut), cubed

2 lbs (or 2, 12-16 oz packs) andouille or *smoked sausage

1/4 cup vegetable oil

1/2 cup white onion, diced

1 stalk celery, diced

1 tbsp Creole seasoning

1/4 tsp cayenne pepper

3/4 cup canned chopped tomatoes, drained

2 tbsp roux

1 tbsp minced garlic

1/4 tsp basil

2 tbsp parsley

2 stalks (about 1 tbsp) green onion, diced

2 cups uncooked rice

5 cups water

Servings: 6-8

Prep Time: 10 minutes
Cook Time: 105 minute

In a large, heavy-bottomed pot over medium-high heat, heat vegetable oil. Season chicken with 1 tbsp Creole seasoning. Add chicken, cayenne, white onions, and celery; then sauté for 10 minutes. Add 5 cups water. Raise heat to high and bring to a boil. Then, lower heat to low-medium. Cover and cook for 30 minutes, stirring every 15 minutes. Add roux and blend until melted; then add tomatoes, basil, and garlic. Raise temperature to high and bring to a boil for 3 minutes. Add rice and then reduce heat to low, simmering for 40-45 minutes, or until rice is cooked and most of the water is absorbed. While simmering, in a small skillet, cook sausage according to package directions. Drain oil from sausage by placing on paper towels. Cut sausage into one-half inch slices. Add sausage, green onions and parsley; blend well into mixture with a metal cooking spoon (wooden spoons tend to mush the rice). Let sit 5 minutes before serving.

Chicken and sausage can be substituted with Pork and giblets for a traditional Jambalaya. Replace chicken in recipe with pork butt and giblets, both cut into cubes, omitting sausage at the end. Beef sausage can also be substituted for pork sausage if you don't eat pork. Personally, I prefer smoked beef sausage.

Simple Smoked Chicken

One of the very popular Friday night rituals in Louisiana during fall time is high school football. All three of the St. Martin Parish high schools are fierce rivals. Breaux Bridge, Cecilia, and St. Martinville High Schools have high football game attendance for every game. It seemed as if the entire Parish was at one of the high schools cheering on sons, cousins, neighbors, and friends alike. I was a cheerleader at Breaux Bridge High School throughout my high school years. The excitement of fall was always something to look forward to every year. Even now, hearing the Breaux Bridge High entrance song, Eye of the Tiger, gives me a burst of energy. On Thursday afternoons, the cheerleaders would gather in a gym room to paint vivid banners to hang around town and at the football stadium. Our signs would taunt the opposing team using their school slogans in a different context. The signs also brightly cheered on our BBHS Tigers. In the early evening hours, the men of our booster club would hold a BBQ for our football players and cheerleaders. You can't get a better BBQ meal from anywhere else than from a group of Louisiana men. We would line up eager to get a plate to eat on the football bleachers. After our meals, the cheerleaders took turns hosting sleepovers. We would watch our favorite teen shows, then head out to "decorate" our favorite football players lawns with toilet paper. Then, we'd drive up and down our Main street, grabbing a bite to eat at a local place. Before heading back to our sleepover, we hung banners aimed at the other teams down the route that they had to take to get to our high school. Sometimes, our local police would assist us in hanging the banners. These are some of my most cherished memories from my youth.

Chicken, cut into pieces (breasts, thighs, legs, wings)

Creole seasoning

Jack Miller's BBQ Sauce® (or your favorite BBQ sauce)

Smoker (preferable) or Grill

Smoker pellets (Hickory or Mesquite) or charcoal

Servings: 4-6

Prep Time: 5 minutes
Inactive: 10 minutes
Cook Time: 85 minutes

Start smoker or grill on high. Season chicken liberally with Creole seasoning and coat lightly with Jack Miller's ® or other BBQ sauce. Cover and refrigerate until smoker or grill is heated. When smoker or grill reaches temperature, place chicken on rack for smoker or indirectly from heat for grill. Lid should remain closed unless turning chicken. Sear chicken on both sides, 5 minutes per side. Then, lower temperature to 325 or medium for 15 minutes. Lower temperature again to smoke or lowest grill setting. Smoke/grill for 50-60 additional minutes. Adjust time as needed. Chicken temperature must be a minimum of 165 at thickest part of breast or thigh. Remove chicken from smoker/grill, cover with foil, and let rest 10 minutes before serving.

Smothered Chicken

1 Chicken, cut into pieces (breasts, thighs, legs, wings)

1 package chicken hearts (may be omitted if desired)

1/4 cup flour

1/8 cup vegetable oil

1 small white onion, diced

1 small green bell pepper, diced

Creole seasoning

Black pepper

1/2 tsp Kitchen Bouquet Browning & Seasoning Sauce®

1/2 cup red wine, preferably a Cabernet Sauvignon

1 whole bay leaf

1 tsp cornstarch

Parsley for garnish

3-4 cups cooked white rice

Servings: 4-6

Prep Time: 10 minutes
Cook Time: 1 hour

Season chicken and hearts liberally with 1 tbsp Creole seasoning. In a heavy bottomed pot, heat vegetable oil on medium heat. Add chicken and hearts to pot, pour Kitchen Bouquet® evenly over chicken/hearts, and brown on all sides over medium-high heat. Add white onions and bell pepper and sauté.   Slowly pour wine over chicken/hearts to deglaze pot.   Add water to pot, covering poultry about 3 inches higher than poultry. Add bay leaf and bring to boil. Lower temperature to medium heat. Remove bay leaf after 2 minutes and discard. Lower temperature again to low-medium heat. Cover and Simmer chicken/hearts over low-medium heat for 40 minutes, stirring frequently, paying attention to scraping the bottom of the pot. Check water levels during cooking time.   Add 3/4 cup flour, 1 tsp cornstarch, and 1 tsp black pepper to a dish or glass and add one cup cold water. Stir until blended well with no lumps. Slowly add to pot to make a gravy. Continue cooking for 10 more minutes. Let sit for 10-15 minutes for gravy to thicken. Serve over rice, season with black pepper, and garnish with parsley.

51

Smothered Okra, Chicken & Shrimp

*2 lbs fresh okra, rinsed, uncut (or frozen okra)

1 lb boneless, skinless chicken thighs, cut into cubes

1/2 lb small raw shrimp

1/8 cup green bell pepper, diced

1 can diced tomatoes, drained

1 medium white onion, diced

1/2 tsp minced garlic

1/4 tsp black pepper

Creole seasoning

White vinegar

Vegetable oil

Tabasco®

Water - on standby for quick use

Servings: 4-6

Prep Time: 20 minutes
Cook Time: 2 hours, 30 minutes

Put fresh okra in a large colander and rinse with water. Immediately rinse okra with vinegar and let sit to allow to dry. Cut fresh okra in one half inch slices with sharp knife, discarding tops and ends of okra.   In a heavy bottomed pot with lid, heat 1 tbsp vegetable oil over high heat. Add fresh okra and allow to sear slightly for 10 minutes, turning carefully. For frozen okra, add okra to pot and 2 tbsp white vinegar; sear for 15 minutes. Stir frequently. Quickly add 1 tbsp water, bell pepper, and onions & sauté for 5 minutes. Add tomatoes, garlic, black pepper, 1 ½ tbsp Creole seasoning, and a dash of Tabasco® Continue cooking on high for 7-8 minutes, stirring occasionally and being sure to scrape the bottom of the pot. Add 1 cup water, stir well and lower heat to medium. Cover and continue cooking for 10 minutes, stirring frequently.   Season chicken thighs with 1 tbsp Creole seasoning. In a separate skillet, add 1/2 tbsp vegetable oil and slightly brown chicken thighs. Transfer browned thighs to okra pot. Blend together. Add 3 cups water; stir; cover and continue cooking over medium heat for 25 minutes, stirring frequently (every 5 minutes).   Add another 3 cups of water and stir well, remembering to scrape the bottom of the pot. Wait 2 minutes, then reduce heat to low-medium. Re-cover and continue cooking for 70-80 minutes, or until nearly all of the water has cooked down. During cooking process, stir four times (every 20 minutes). Just before adding shrimp, raise temperature to high heat, uncover, and stir for 2 minutes. Lower temperature back to medium. Season shrimp liberally with Creole seasoning and add to pot. Stir, cover, and continue cooking 10 minutes. Serve over rice as a meal or without rice as a side for a meal. I like to eat this dish a bit spicy, so for my personal plate, I add more Creole seasoning and Tabasco®

*If you are unable to find fresh okra, frozen cut okra may be substituted. Pay attention to the start of the recipe, as fresh or frozen will be started differently.

Smothered Pork Chops

Pack (4-6) of bone-in pork chops (regular cut)

1 small white onion, diced

1 small green bell pepper, diced

1 small red bell pepper, diced

1/2 clove garlic, minced

1/2 tbsp Vegetable oil

3/4 cup flour

2 tsp cornstarch

Flour for sprinkling

Creole seasoning

Kitchen Bouquet Browning & Seasoning Sauce®

Water

Servings: 4-6

Prep Time: 10 minutes
Cook Time: 90 minutes

In a heavy bottomed pot with lid, heat vegetable oil over medium-high heat. Season pork chops with Creole seasoning and Kitchen Bouquet.® Lightly sprinkle a bit of flour over both sides of pork chops and add to pot, browning on both sides. Lower temperature to medium heat. Sauté onions and bell peppers; then add garlic. Add water to cover pork chops 1 inch higher than chops. Bring to a boil and allow to continue boiling, stirring frequently, for 5 minutes. Stir and lower temperature to low-medium heat. Cover and simmer for 60 minutes, adding water if needed. Add ¾ cup flour, 2 tsp cornstarch, and ½ tsp Kitchen Bouquet® to a bowl, then add one cup cold water. Whisk until blended well with no lumps. Slowly add to pot to make a gravy. Continue cooking and stirring for 10 more minutes or until gravy has formed. Let sit for 10-15 minutes for gravy to thicken. Serve over rice.

Smothered Hamburger Steak

1 lb lean ground beef
1 small onion, diced
1 small green bell pepper; half diced, half cut in thin strips
1 egg yolk
1 whole bay leaf
1 slice white bread, crumbled
1/4 tsp minced garlic
1/2 tsp roux
1/2 tsp Worcestershire sauce
1 tsp Kitchen Bouquet Browning & Seasoning Sauce®
1/2 tbsp Creole seasoning + extra
1 tbsp cornstarch
1 tbsp vegetable oil
Water for cooking
Black for sprinkling
Flour for sprinkling
1/3 cup flour for gravy

Servings: 4-6

Prep Time: 10 minutes
Inactive: 15 minutes
Cook Time: 1 hour

In a large mixing bowl, add ground beef, ½ of the diced onion, diced bell pepper, egg yolk, crumbled white bread, garlic, Worcestershire sauce, Kitchen Bouquet,® and ½ tbsp Creole seasoning. Mix well. Form 4-6 patties in rounds (like a hamburger patty) and place on a plate or dish. Cover and put in freezer for 10-15 minutes to set. Meanwhile, heat vegetable oil over medium heat. Add remaining ½ diced onions and strips of bell pepper to large, wide pan with lid and sauté. Remove patties from freezer, lightly sprinkle flour over patties, then add to pan, browning on both sides for 3 minutes each.

If there are bits of meat that have formed around patties because patties did not set properly, remove patties from pan, along with any onions or bell pepper strips that can be removed. Place all on a plate. Discard anything remaining in pan and scrub pan clean. Return patties and add additional onions and bell pepper. Add patties back to pan. Continue with recipe.

Add roux and allow to melt. Add 2 cups of water and carefully stir, avoiding touching the patties. Cover with lid, lower stove to low heat. Simmer on low for 45 minutes; checking water temperature does not go below patties (add small amounts of water as necessary). In a glass or small dish, add 1/3 cup flour, cornstarch, and 1/2 tsp Creole seasoning, then add 1 cup cold water and blend until there are no lumps. Slowly pour into pan and stir carefully; avoiding touching patties. Raise heat to medium and continue cooking 10 minutes. Garnish with black pepper and parsley; serve over rice.

Baked Chicken stuffed w/ Shrimp Dressing

The very first meal that I attempted to cook as a teenager was baked chicken. This may seem ambitious, but I was very hungry and no one else was at home. I searched the refrigerator and we didn't have anything I wanted. Next, I opened the freezer in hopes of finding something to pop in the microwave. NOTHING!! So, there it laid – a whole frozen chicken. With every ounce of confidence in the World, I took the frozen whole chicken out of the freezer and turned on the oven. I grabbed a baking dish, some Creole seasoning, and slathered the chicken with seasoning. Then I popped the chicken in the oven – not even yet heated for baking. I don't remember how long I baked the chicken, but it was hours. At that point, my mission overtook my sense of hunger. So, I baked that chicken…frozen, giblets still in plastic and all. I ate my chicken with all the pride of a genuine success. My Mom came home to see what I'd done. She was in awe at my naivety and helpless cooking skills. Decades later, my Mom still laughs at my frozen chicken. Needless to say, I've more than caught up on cooking. I hope you'll enjoy!

1 whole roasting chicken, giblets removed	1/4 cup green bell pepper, diced
Creole seasoning for sprinkling	2 tsp chopped parsley
Mayonnaise for basting	1/2 tsp diced garlic
1/4 lb small raw shrimp, cut into pieces	1 tbsp Creole seasoning
1 package cornbread mix	1/3 cup chicken stock
1/4 cup white onion, diced	2 tbsp melted butter
1/4 cup celery, diced	1/3 cup boiled water

Servings: 4-6

Prep Time: 10 minute

Cook Time: 80 minute

Start with making cornbread. Follow package directions, plus add all veggies (onion, bell pepper, celery, parsley, garlic), and 1 tsp Creole seasoning to bake into cornbread mix. Cool cornbread. After cornbread has baked, preheat oven to 450.

In a large mixing bowl, crumble cooled cornbread mixture; then, add melted butter, and raw shrimp. Mix thoroughly. Ensure giblets are out of chicken cavity. Liberally season outside of chicken with Creole Seasoning, and then spread mayonnaise around whole chicken. Loosely stuff chicken cavity with shrimp stuffing, being careful not to overstuff. Place chicken, breasts down, in roasting pan. Bake in 450 oven for 10 minutes. Then, lower oven temperature to 350 and continue baking 22 minutes per pound of whole chicken listed on package (22 x lbs listed). *Halfway through 350 cooking time, add 1/3 cup boiled water around chicken in roasting pan. *30 minutes before cooking time ends baste chicken with liquid in roaster. Insert meat thermometer into thickest part of thigh, away from the bone, to ensure chicken is at least 165 degrees. Continue cooking until chicken reaches safe temperature. Let chicken rest for 15 minutes after removing from oven.

Filet Mignon topped w/ Jumbo Lump Crab & Cream Sauce

4-6 Center cut filet mignon

1 tbsp butter, thinly sliced into one slice per filet

Black pepper

Himalayan pink salt or table salt

Cast iron skillet or large, heavy skillet/pan

Glass lid smaller than skillet

Cream sauce:

1 cup heavy whipping cream

16 oz jumbo lump crab

3 tbsp flour

4 tbsp butter

1/2 tbsp black pepper

1/2 tsp salt

1/2 tsp cayenne pepper

Servings: 4-6

Prep Time: 10 minutes
Inactive: 10 minutes
Cook Time: 40 minutes

*Cookbook Add In: Suggestion guide for 1-inch filet:
Medium (pink center): Initial 5 minutes per side, plus 2 minutes per side (my personal preference)
Medium Well (some pink): Initial 5 minutes per side, plus 3-4 minutes per side
Well Done (no pink): Initial 5 minutes per side, plus 8-10 minutes per side

	RARE 135°F/57°C	MEDIUM-RARE 145°F/63°C	MEDIUM 160°F/71°C	MEDIUM-WELL 165°F/74°C
¼ inch	45 seconds	1 minute	2 minutes	3 minutes
½ inch	3 minutes	4 minutes	5 minutes	6 minutes
¾ inch	4 to 5 minutes	6 to 7 minutes	8 to 10 minutes	10 to 12 minutes
1 inch	8 to 10 minutes	10 to 12 minutes	12 to 14 minutes	14 to 16 minutes
1½ inches	14 to 16 minutes	16 to 19 minutes	22 to 26 minutes	26 to 30 minutes
2 inches	18 to 22 minutes	24 to 28 minutes	28 to 32 minutes	33 to 36 minutes

In a pan, heat butter over medium heat. Add 3 tbsp flour and stir well. Continue stirring for 5 minutes, until smooth and blended well. Slowly stir in heavy whipping cream, black pepper, cayenne, and salt. Stir until blended. Add crabmeat and cook for 3-4 minutes. Let stand, stirring occasionally. Re-heat on low after cooking filet, while they are resting.

Place filets on plate and season with Himalayan salt or salt and pepper. Let filets sit out at room temperature for 10 minutes. Meanwhile, heat large cast iron skillet or large skillet over medium-high heat. When skillet is very hot, sear filets in skillet for 5 minutes per side, placing glass lid over filets (lid should lay on top of fillets, not rest on edges of skillet, covering 3/4 of skillet). Lower temperature to medium and cook based on chart above based on thickness of filet and desired doneness, turning filet halfway through cooking time. Remove lid using potholder and raise temperature back to high. Rotate filets on their sides and quickly sear all sides of filets. Transfer filets to platter and pat each with thin slice of butter. Let rest for 5 minutes. Pour sauce over filet and serve immediately.

Buttermilk Fried Chicken

1 fryer chicken, cut in pieces (breasts, thighs, legs, wings)

32 oz buttermilk

2 eggs, beaten

1/4 tsp black pepper

2 tsp white pepper

Self rising flour

Creole seasoning for seasoning

Vegetable or peanut oil for frying

Servings: 4-6

Prep Time: 10 minutes
Inactive: 12-24 hours
Cook Time: 30 minutes

Season chicken liberally with Creole seasoning. In large bowl, mix buttermilk and eggs. Add chicken to bowl, making sure all pieces are thoroughly covered in buttermilk mixture. Cover and refrigerate 12-24 hours. In large, heavy pot (with available cover), add vegetable oil; filling 1/3 of pot. Heat over medium-high heat. Meanwhile, remove marinated chicken from refrigerator. Add self rising flour to large food storage bag or separate large bowl and season with Creole seasoning and black & white pepper. One by one, add chicken pieces; shaking bag to cover chicken thoroughly after each piece. This will need to be done in batches to not overcrowd chicken. After a few pieces, place coated chicken on platter until process is complete. Allow chicken to sit for 15 minutes, in order to set batter. Check oil by putting a pinch of dry flour in pot. If it sizzles, you're ready to fry. Slowly add chicken to hot oil. Fry for 10 minutes, then carefully turn chicken pieces once. Cover pot with lid after turning chicken. Lower temperature to just below medium and fry covered for 15 additional minutes. Carefully remove lid, turn chicken pieces, and raise temperature to high; frying for an additional 5-6 minutes. Chicken breast should be 165 degrees when measured from thickest part. Remove chicken, one by one, onto paper towel lined platter for draining.

Buttermilk Wings & Red Velvet Waffles

1 dozen chicken wings

16 oz buttermilk

2 eggs, beaten

Creole seasoning for seasoning

1/4 tsp black pepper

2 tsp white pepper

Self rising flour

Vegetable or peanut oil for frying

Waffles:

Waffle mix, **<u>plus</u>** ingredients listed on box

Red velvet cake mix

1 tsp vanilla extract

Waffle maker

Servings: 4-6

Prep Time: 15 minutes
Inactive: 12-24 hours
Cook Time: 30 minutes

Season chicken liberally with Creole seasoning. In large bowl, mix buttermilk and eggs. Add chicken to bowl, making sure all pieces are thoroughly seasoned and covered in buttermilk mixture. Cover and refrigerate 12-24 hours. Remove marinated chicken from refrigerator. Add self rising flour to large food storage bag or separate large bowl and season liberally with 1 tbsp Creole seasoning and black & white pepper. One by one, add chicken pieces; shaking bag to cover chicken thoroughly after each piece. This will need to be done in batches to not overcrowd chicken. After a few pieces, place coated chicken on platter until process is complete. Allow chicken to sit for 15 minutes, in order to set batter. Meanwhile, fill pot 1/3 with oil and heat on medium-high heat. When heated, carefully fry chicken wings in batches until golden brown, making sure not to overcrowd pot. Drain on paper towel lined plate or platter.

In a mixing bowl, follow waffle mix directions, **EXCEPT** replace 1/3 of waffle mix for desired amount with red velvet cake mix. Add vanilla extract and continue following mix directions. Pour batter into waffle maker and cook according to waffle maker instructions. Serve with chicken wings.

Sides:

Fiery sunset over Lake Martin Photo Courtesy: Docq Gaspard /CDG Images

Shutterstock

Shutterstock

Cajun Potato Salad

Oh, potato salad. This is a common side for Cajun and Creole dishes. So many versions of potato salad exist around the World. Some are made plain with only potatoes and mustard, while others are chocked full of raisins, apples, nuts, or relish. I traditionally made my potato salad the way I'd eaten it all my life – with potatoes, eggs, mayonnaise, mustard, seasoning, and sometimes relish. As I was making dinner one night, I realized that I was out of relish. We lived about 20-30 minutes to the closest grocery store. So, I scoured my refrigerator for a substitute. The only green condiment I had was a jar of green olives. Well, it was worth a try. I chopped up the olives about the size of pieces of relish and threw them in the mix. The taste was different, but had a nice, subtle tang. I realized that the sweetness of relish didn't compliment my potato salad as well as the olives. So, my traditional Cajun potato salad is now as tangy and sassy as I am. Feel free to omit the olives, but it's a favorite amongst my two besties, Bridget and Susan. I suggest that you give it a try!

3 red potatoes, washed, peeled, and cut in quarters

1 red potato, washed and cut in quarters (not peeled)

3 boiled eggs, peeled and mashed

2 cooked yolks only from boiled eggs

1/2 cup mayonnaise

2 tbsp yellow mustard

1/2 tsp Creole seasoning

1/4 tsp Black pepper

Paprika for seasoning

1/2 tbsp diced Spanish Pimiento Stuffed Manzanilla green olives (optional)

Servings: 4-6

Prep Time: 5 minutes
Inactive: 25 minutes
Cook Time: 20 minutes

Boil potatoes over high heat in stock pot until tender, approximately 15-20 minutes. Remove potatoes from pot and immediately place in mixing bowl. Allow potatoes to steam dry for approximately 10 minutes. Season lightly with ½ tsp Creole seasoning and ¼ tsp black pepper. Add 3 mashed eggs and 2 egg yolks to potatoes. Mix well, slightly mashing everything. Add mustard, mayonnaise, and green olives. Mix well, ensuring that the texture is smooth, all ingredients are mixed in, there a few lumps, and there are no large chunks of potato. Cover and refrigerate until ready to serve. If you are planning on serving soon, cover and put bowl in freezer for a minimum of 15 minutes before serving. This potato salad is best served cold. Lightly sprinkle paprika for garnish before serving.

Creamed Spinach

2 packages frozen spinach

1/4 cup aged white cheddar, cut into small squares

1/3 cup smoked Gouda, cut into small squares

1/2 cup sharp cheddar, cut into small squares

3 slices American cheese, cut into strips

Shredded cheddar for topping

1/4 cup heavy whipping cream

1 tbsp butter

1 tsp minced garlic

1/8 cup diced onion

2 tsp Creole seasoning

Cheesecloth

Servings: 4-6

Prep Time: 15 minutes
Cook Time: 45 minutes

Preheat oven to 350.

Put frozen spinach in large, microwaveable dish. Microwave on high for 5 minutes; stir; continue microwaving for 3 minutes. Remove from microwave and strain remaining water from spinach using cheesecloth (or paper towels pressing the spinach in the dish to remove excess water). Add Creole seasoning, cheeses (**except** shredded cheddar), heavy cream, garlic, onions, and butter. Mix well. Bake for 30 minutes, stirring halfway through cooking time. Sprinkle shredded cheddar over dish. Set on broil for 3-5 minutes, until shredded cheese is melted and slightly golden brown. Serve with Tortilla or Pita chips.

Corn Maque Choux Cups

2 dozen frozen mini pie shells

10 oz package frozen corn

1/4 cup yellow onion, diced

1/8 cup green bell pepper, diced

1 cup heavy cream

4 tbsp butter

2 tbsp corn starch

1 tbsp melted butter

1 tsp black pepper

1 tsp salt

Servings: 2 dozen

Prep Time: 10 minutes
Cook Time: 40 minutes

Prepare or preheat pie shells according to package directions for filling pies. Remove from oven. Baste with melted butter.

Preheat oven to 400 degrees.

In a pot over medium heat, melt 4 tbsp butter. Sauté onions and bell pepper for 8-10 minutes, until tender. Stir in cornstarch and blend until smooth. Add frozen corn and heavy cream, black pepper, and salt. Continue cooking for 10-15 minutes, stirring frequently until thickened.

Pour corn mixture into pie shells and bake in preheated oven for 10 minutes, until mixture is bubbling. Serve warm.

Rice Dressing

Rice dressing is another Cajun and Creole side staple. In Louisiana, "Plate lunches" are extremely popular options for both takeout and sit-down meals. Plate lunches are generously sized and compromised of a meat, poultry, or seafood item and two to three side options. Quite often, rice dressing is automatically included as a side. Other side options are usually potato salad, baked beans, green beans, or green salad. Main dishes usually change daily and are rotated weekly.

1 lb lean ground beef

1/2 lb ground pork

1/2 lb raw chicken livers, diced

1 small white onion, diced

1 small green bell pepper, diced

1/2 bunch (about ½ cup) fresh parsley, diced

1 stalk green onion, diced

1 tbsp Creole seasoning

1 tsp black pepper

1 1/2 tbsp roux

1/2 tsp vegetable oil

6 cups cooked rice

Water

Servings: 8-10

Prep Time: 15 minutes
Cook Time: 45 minutes

In a large pan, heat vegetable oil over medium-high heat. Season all meat liberally with 1 tbsp Creole seasoning. Add ground beef, ground pork, and chicken livers to pot and brown, stirring frequently for 10 minutes. Drain most of the oil. Lower temperature to medium. Add black pepper, onions, and bell pepper and continue cooking for 10 minutes. Quickly melt roux into pot, begin adding water until all meat is covered above 1 inch. Raise temperature to high and bring to a boil, then lower temperature to medium-low, simmering for 20 minutes, stirring occasionally. Add water if necessary; however most of the water will need to cook down until meat is just moist. Add cooked rice, green onions, and parsley; mixing well. Compact rice dressing so that it may steam off any excess water. Serve immediately or warm.

Cornbread Dressing

Servings: 8-10

Prep Time: 20 minutes
Cook Time: 90 minutes

1 lb lean ground beef
1/2 lb ground pork
1/2 lb raw chicken livers, diced
1 large white onion, diced
1 large green bell pepper, diced
2 stalks celery, diced
1/2 bunch fresh parsley, diced
1/2 stalk green onion, diced
1 tbsp Creole seasoning
1 tsp Creole seasoning
1 tsp Black pepper
1 1/2 tbsp roux
4 tbsp melted butter
4, 8.5-9 oz packages cornbread mix and ingredients listed on package
1 cup garlic croutons, slightly crushed
1 cup chicken or turkey stock (if baking chicken or turkey, try to use some of stock from it)

Make cornbread mix, according to package directions*; except adding 1/4 cup diced onion, 1/4 cup green bell pepper, 1/2 of the diced celery, and 1 tsp Creole seasoning (per package) to the mixes.

*Increase cooking time by 8-10 minutes to accommodate multiple packages baking at once. Carefully watch that cornbread does not overbrown when increasing cooking time.

Preheat oven to 350.

In a large pan, heat pot over medium-high heat. Season all meat lightly with 1 tbsp Creole seasoning. Add ground beef and ground pork to pot to slightly brown (about 8 minutes), stirring frequently. Add chicken liver; and remaining onions, bell pepper, and celery. Continue cooking for 10 minutes. Quickly melt roux into pot and begin adding water until all meat is covered above 1 inch. Bring to a boil, then lower temperature to medium-low, simmering for 20 minutes, stirring occasionally. Add water if necessary; however most of the water will need to cook down until meat is just moist. Break up cornbread into big crumbles, but do NOT mash down, with a large spoon.   In a large roasting pan, add baked cornbread, croutons, melted butter, 1 tbsp Creole seasoning, green onions, parsley, and black pepper. Mix and blend well until uniform. Add meat mixture. Then, slowly pour chicken or turkey stock evenly over mixture; ensuring that the mixture is very moist, but not watered down. Do not use all stock if mixture looks like it will have too much liquid. Mix well again, making sure there are no dry spots. Bake in oven for 40-45 minutes, stirring twice during baking time. Check cornbread during baking time to ensure that it is not browning or drying out. Cornbread dressing should be slightly moist, but not wet. Serve warm.

Seafood Oyster & Shrimp Dressing

1 container 16 oz oysters, drained

-Note: You may double shrimp if you don't care for oysters-

1 lb medium raw shrimp, peeled and deveined

2, 8.5-9 oz packages cornbread mix and ingredients listed on package

1 cup garlic croutons, slightly crushed

1 cup white onion, diced

1 cup green bell pepper, diced

2 stalks celery, diced

5 tbsp fresh parsley, diced

1 stalk green onion, diced

1/4 tsp cayenne pepper

Creole seasoning

Black pepper

2 tbsp roux

4 tbsp melted butter

2 tbsp vegetable oil

1/2 cup chicken or seafood stock

Servings: 6-8

Prep Time: 20 minutes
Cook Time: 80 minutes

Make cornbread mix, according to package directions*; except adding 1 tsp (per cornbread package) Creole seasoning, 1/4 cup diced onion, 1/4 cup green bell pepper, and 1/2 of the diced celery to the mixes.   *Increase cooking time by 8-10 minutes to accommodate multiple packages baking at once. Carefully watch that cornbread does not overbrown when increasing cooking time.

Preheat oven to 350.

In a sauté pan, heat 2 tbsp vegetable oil over medium-high heat. Add remaining ¾ cup each onion, bell pepper, celery; cayenne pepper; and 1 tsp Creole seasoning. Sauté 5-6 minutes, until tender. Break up cornbread into big crumbles, but do <u>NOT</u> mash down, with a large spoon. In a roasting pan, add dry ingredients first: baked cornbread, croutons, sautéed veggies, 1 tsp Creole seasoning, and ¼ tsp black pepper. Then add chicken/seafood stock and butter. Mix and blend well until uniform; making sure there are no dry spots. The mixture will be very moist.   Bake in oven for 20 minutes, stirring twice. Season shrimp and oysters with ½ tsp each with Creole seasoning. Remove pan from oven. Mix seafood, parsley, and green onions into cornbread mixture and continue baking in oven for 30 minutes, stirring (carefully rotating bottom of mixture to top) halfway through baking time. Serve immediately or warm.

Sautéed Cabbage and Ham

1 large head of cabbage, rinsed, trimmed, and cut into three-inch strips;

(discard top and bottom of cabbage head)

2 ham steaks, cut into small one-half inch cubes

Servings: 6-8

4 slices uncooked bacon

1 small white onion, diced

Prep Time: 10 minutes
Cook Time: 45 minutes

1 tbsp Creole seasoning

1 tsp black pepper

1 cup water

In a large, heavy bottom stock pot (with available lid for later) over medium heat, cook bacon until fat renders, but is not crispy. Add diced onion and pre-cut ham steaks to bacon drippings and sauté for 5-6 minutes, until onion is tender. Add cabbage, Creole seasoning, and black pepper to pot and sauté for 15 minutes, stirring frequently. Stir in water. Cover with lid and continue cooking for 15 minutes, until water has cooked down. Finished dish should not have any water remaining. Serve over rice or as a side dish.

Sautéed Brussels Sprouts w/ Bacon

3 cups fresh brussel sprouts, rinsed & dried

3 slices raw thick cut bacon, chopped

2 tbsp melted butter

1/2 lemon wedge

Salt for seasoning

Black Pepper for seasoning

Grated parmesan cheese for sprinkling (about 2 tbsp)

Freshly cut lemon

Aluminum foil

Servings: 4-6

Prep Time: 10 minutes
Cook Time: 40 minutes

Preheat oven to 400.

In a microwave safe bowl, add 1 tbsp water to brussel sprouts and microwave on high for 3 minutes. Transfer brussel sprouts to glass or stoneware baking dish. Add uncooked bacon and gently mix well so that bacon is evenly distributed amongst brussel sprouts. Pour melted butter over food and lightly season evenly with salt and black pepper. Cover loosely with aluminum foil. Bake in preheated oven for 30 minutes, stirring twice (every 15 minutes). With baking dish remaining on middle rack in oven, evenly sprinkle parmesan cheese. Remove aluminum foil and discard. Turn oven on broil and, watching carefully, broil until parmesan is a golden brown. Remove dish from oven and serve immediately, spritzing lemon over dish.

Bacon Wrapped Asparagus

1 bunch large asparagus, rinsed well with bottoms cut off

1 slice of uncooked bacon per asparagus spear

2 wooden toothpicks per asparagus spear

Black pepper for seasoning

Garlic powder for seasoning

2 tbsp unsalted butter, melted

Servings: 4-6

Prep Time: 15 minutes
Cook Time: 30 minutes

Preheat oven to 375.

Using a platter, lay asparagus spears into rows. Take a slice of bacon and stretch and wrap it diagonally around an asparagus spear. Secure bacon below the tip of the spear and above the bottom of the spear with toothpicks. Repeat with remaining spears and bacon. Sprinkle bacon-wrapped spears lightly with garlic powder and black pepper. Lay asparagus spears flat in a single line around a large baking dish. Pour melted butter over asparagus spears. Cover loosely with aluminum foil to prevent splattering. Bake in preheated oven for 30 minutes, or until bacon is crisp. Serve warm as a side.

Southern Collard Greens

2 large bunches fresh collard greens. Wash well, dry, remove middle stems, and cut into three-inch squares

2-3 smoked ham hocks

5 slices applewood smoked thick bacon, uncooked

1/4 cup apple cider vinegar

1 medium white onion, diced

1 tsp minced garlic

2 tsp black pepper

1 tsp cayenne pepper

2 tbsp Creole seasoning

1/2 tsp red pepper flakes

Vegetable oil

Water

Servings: 6-8

Prep Time: 15 minutes
Cook Time: 90 minutes

In a large, heavy bottomed skillet, heat bacon until fat renders and bacon is just cooked (not crispy). Remove bacon from skillet, cut into one-half inch pieces with kitchen scissors, and set on a plate (do not drain). In skillet with bacon drippings, add 1 tsp vegetable oil and brown ham hocks on all sides. Transfer to plate with bacon. In the same skillet, add onion and sauté for 5 minutes over medium-high heat. Slowly add Creole seasoning, black pepper, cayenne pepper, garlic, and apple cider vinegar. Mix well and remove skillet from heat. Transfer all contents of skillet into large stock pot over high heat. Immediately add collard greens to stock pot. Stir all ingredients together until blended well. Quickly begin adding water to stock pot until all greens are covered, leaving at least 3 inches to the top of pot. Stir well and bring to a boil. Lower heat to medium and cook for 1 hour, stirring frequently and adding water, if necessary, up until the last 15 minutes. All water should be cooked out before finishing. Sprinkle red pepper flakes and mix well. Serve hot as a side.

Homemade Mac 'n Cheese

8 oz (half of 1 lb package) Elbow macaroni

4 tbsp butter

1 cup half & half

1/2 cup heavy whipping cream

1/2 cup shredded sharp cheddar

2 cups sharp cheddar, cut into small pieces

2 oz (1/4 cup) white cheddar, cut into small pieces

2 oz (1/4 cup) medium cheddar, cut into small pieces

6 slices American cheese

1 tbsp Ricotta cheese

1 tbsp flour

1 egg yolk

1 tsp Black pepper

1 tsp salt

Servings: 6-8

Prep Time: 10 minutes
Cook Time: 60 minutes

Preheat oven to 350 degrees.

Bring 6 cups water to a boil in large pot on stove. Stir in elbow macaroni and boil for 8 minutes (or time listed on package). Remove from heat and drain. In pot, add 4 tbsp butter and melt over medium heat. When melted, add flour and stir until smooth. Add heavy cream, half & half, black pepper, and salt. Stir until blended. Add all cheeses **except** ½ cup shredded cheddar and continue stirring. Stir and cook for additional 8-10 minutes, until smooth. Turn off stove burner and add egg yolk, mixing well. Transfer contents into large baking dish. Bake in preheated oven for 20 minutes. Sprinkle ½ cup shredded cheddar cheese on top. Turn oven on high broil – do **NOT** move oven rack up. Watching carefully (do **NOT** walk away from oven); broil for 3-4 minutes or until golden, bubbling brown. Remove from oven IMMEDIATELY. Let rest for 10 minutes. Serve with your favorite dish.

Crawfish or Lobster Mac 'n Cheese

, 6-8 oz lobster tails, meat removed from shell OR 1 lb crawfish tails

oz (half of 1 lb package) Elbow macaroni

tbsp butter

cup half & half

/2 cup heavy whipping cream

cups shredded sharp cheddar

/2 cup shredded sharp cheddar

oz (1/4 cup) white cheddar, cut into small pieces

oz (1/4 cup) medium cheddar, cut into small pieces

oz (1/4 cup) smoked gouda

slices American cheese

tbsp Ricotta cheese

tbsp flour

egg yolk

tbsp Creole seasoning

½ tsp red chili flakes

tsp Black pepper

tsp White pepper

Servings: 6-8

Prep Time: 10 minutes
Cook Time: 65 minutes

Preheat oven to 350 degrees.

Bring 6 cups water to a boil in large pot on stove. Stir in elbow macaroni and boil for 8 minutes (or me listed on package). Remove from heat and drain. In pot, add 4 tbsp butter and melt over medium eat. When melted, add flour and stir until smooth. Add heavy cream, half & half, black pepper, and white pepper. Stir until blended. Add all cheeses **except** ½ cup shredded cheddar and continue stirring. Stir and cook for additional 8-10 minutes, until smooth. Turn off stove burner and add egg olk, mixing well. Transfer contents into large baking dish. Bake in preheated oven for 15 minutes. Season lobster or crawfish with Creole seasoning and red pepper flakes. Stir in lobster or crawfish. Sprinkle ½ cup shredded cheddar cheese on top. Continue cooking for 10 minutes. Turn oven on igh broil – do **NOT** move oven rack up. Watching carefully (do **NOT** walk away from oven); broil for -4 minutes or until golden, bubbling brown. Remove from oven IMMEDIATELY. Let rest for 10 minutes. Serve with your favorite dish.

Extras:

Purple Gallinule Photo courtesy: Cheri Lynn Soileau

Gigi's Homemade Roux

One batch roux

In a heavy-bottomed pot or large cast iron skillet, heat **1 cup oil** and **1 cup flour** over medium heat for 3 minutes, stirring vigorously. Lower temperature to low heat and continue to cook, stirring constantly until mixture is a dark brown color. Do not scrape the sides of pot or skillet. If mixture begins to bubble, remove from heat immediately and allow to cool; return to stove over low heat and continue. If mixture begins to smoke or dark specs appear, remove from heat and discard when cooled. You must start over and adjust temperature to meet your stove's heat output. Start with low-medium heat and decrease to low heat instead. Do not use burned roux. It will ruin any dish you attempt to use it in. If you need time to practice cooking this roux, but you want to try a recipe, I suggest one brand of retail jarred roux. I've found that Ragin Cajun Dark Roux® is the closest commercial brand to my homemade roux. I've even had to use it in a pinch. I haven't tried every brand of roux, but out of the few I have, I feel that this brand is like mine. Roux in a jar is hardened, so I use a heavy tablespoon to scoop it out. Do this before starting to cook. Keep practicing.

Large batch roux

48 oz vegetable oil

5 lb bag of all-purpose flour

In a large crock pot add 48 oz of vegetable oil on highest setting. Let oil heat for 30 minutes. Slowly stir in 5 lbs flour to heated oil. Stir until well mixed. Add more flour if necessary. The texture should resemble a smooth, mixed cake batter. Stir every 30 minutes until roux reaches a dark brown color. Turn off cooker. Allow roux to cool, stirring occasionally. Store roux in several glass jars or containers in freezer. This recipe is the perfect consistency of roux that will allow you to easily spoon out the amount of roux you need directly from the freezer for a recipe. This homemade batch will allow you to make many wonderful dishes.

Brown Gravy

2 tbsp flour

1 tbsp cornstarch mixed with 1 cup cold water

1 cup cold water (additional)

4 tbsp unsalted butter

1 tbsp Creole seasoning

1/4 tsp black pepper

1/4 tsp garlic powder

1/4 tsp onion powder

1 tsp Kitchen Bouquet Browning & Seasoning [®]

Servings: 1 cup gravy

Prep Time: 5 minutes
Cook Time: 15 minutes

In a pot or sauté pan, melt butter over medium heat. Add flour to melted butter and stir for 1 minute. Add all remaining ingredients. Stir constantly until mixture thickens into a gravy, about 10-12 minutes. Remove from heat and allow to thicken further.

Serve over your favorite poultry, pork, or beef dish. You may add in the stock from meat you have cooked to this mixture for a more flavorful gravy along with the cornstarch, water, and seasonings. Replace water with same amount of stock if available.

White Gravy

8 tbsp unsalted butter, cut into pieces for faster melting

2 tbsp bacon grease

1/3 cup flour

3 cups whole milk

1 tsp salt

1/4 tsp black pepper

1/4 tsp white pepper

1/4 tsp Creole seasoning

Servings: 4-6

Prep Time: 5 minutes
Cook Time: 15 minutes

In a medium pot, melt butter over medium heat. Add in bacon grease. Slowly stir in unseasoned flour and stir constantly until mixed well with no lumps for 2 minutes; do not allow to brown. Add salt, black pepper, white pepper, and Creole seasoning to pot. Then, stir in milk until mix well; about 6-8 minutes.   Remove from heat and allow gravy to thicken.

Serve over biscuits, toast, mashed potatoes, or any fried chicken dish.

Cajun Dipping Sauce

Servings: 4-6

Prep Time: 5 minutes
Cook Time: 0

1 cup mayonnaise

1 cup ketchup

1/4 tsp Creole seasoning

1/2 tbsp Cajun Power Garlic Sauce® or 1/2 tbsp Tabasco® & 1/4 tsp garlic powder

Mix ingredients together. This sauce is great a crawfish dip at a crawfish boil. It's also great as a dip for chicken nuggets, chicken tenders, fried catfish nuggets, or your favorite fried seafood.

Seafood Cream Sauce

8 oz jumbo lump crab

1/4 lb small raw shrimp, peeled & deveined

1/4 lb cleaned crawfish tails

3 tbsp flour

3 tbsp butter

1 cup heavy whipping cream

1 ½ cup whole milk

1 tsp Creole seasoning

½ tsp white pepper

Parsley for garnish

Servings: 4-6

Prep Time: 10 minutes
Cook Time: 10 minutes

In a pan, melt butter over medium-high heat. Add 3 tbsp flour and stir well. Continue stirring for 2 minutes, until smooth and blended well. Slowly stir in heavy whipping cream, milk, and Creole seasoning. Lower temperature to medium and stir until blended smooth with no lumps. Add seafood and cook for 3-4 minutes. Turn stove burner off and let stand, stirring occasionally until ready to use.

Desserts & Treats:

Purple Gallinule Photo courtesy: Cheri Lynn Soileau

Shutterstock

Shutterstock

Gâteau du Sirop (Syrup Cake)

1 cup Louisiana Cane Syrup (Steen's® brand is best)

2 1/2 cup flour, 3 tsp baking powder, 1/2 tsp nutmeg, 1/2 tsp cinnamon; all sifted together

2 eggs

1/2 cup unsalted butter

1/2 brown sugar

1/2 cup milk

1 tbsp white vinegar

1 tsp grated orange rind zest

1/2 tsp baking soda

1 tsp vanilla extract

Powdered sugar for dusting

Vegetable oil

Servings: 10-12

Prep Time: 20 minutes
Bake Time: 45 minutes

Preheat oven to 350.

In a large mixing bowl, cream butter and brown sugar together. Add eggs, orange zest, and vanilla extract. Beat well. Slowly pour in flour, syrup, and milk; alternating the three. In a separate small bowl, mix vinegar and baking soda together. Fold into flour mixture in mixing bowl. Lightly coat 8x8 baking pan with vegetable oil, place wax paper over pan; then flip wax paper over, oiled side up. Pour cake mix into pan. Bake for 40-45 minutes in preheated oven. Let cake cool to warm before serving. Dust with powdered sugar.

Pecan Pralines

My Grandparents had a little house on the Bayou Teche in an area called "Promiseland" in Parks, Louisiana. On that land, pecan trees seemingly taller than ten story buildings, bear fruit as hearty and delicious as anyone could ever hope to eat. In Promiseland, generations of people grow into family land. When my Mom was little, these families would band together for wedding celebrations. Each family had a role in the wedding. The bride to be went door to door to invite everyone to the wedding. One favorited family, The Phillips, were preferred cooks for all of Parks, according to my Mom. The women of the couple's families would bake cakes and rest them high on cupboards. Although this was long before my time, I can clearly imagine these wonderful moments of unity. As for my own time in Promiseland, every Fall we'd gather on the vacant land and pick huge pecans that had fallen from the trees. With plentiful bounty, we'd crack pecans to eat, make pecan pies, and make pecan candy a.k.a. pecan pralines. Traditionally, pralines can be difficult to make depending on the level of humidity in the air and in the house. One of the traditional ingredients for making pralines is evaporated milk. The process involves the evaporated milk hardening to form the base of the pralines. When there is too much moisture in the air, the milk remains soft; rendering the pralines a gooey mess. Therefore, praline making is typically reserved for fall and winter seasons. However, through determination and months of trial and error, I developed a recipe that replaces the evaporated milk and allows the pralines to harden in any weather! This recipe may take a bit of practice for some, but my friends that have made it have been successful. I'm sure that you will find this detailed recipe a success as well!

Pecan trees in SW Louisiana Photo courtesy: Main Focus LLC; B&W insert: My Grandparent's house on Bayou Teche in Promiseland, Parks, LA during a rare Louisiana snowfall. Pecan trees towering in the background.

Continued on next page…

Pecan Pralines
...continued

2 cups white sugar

1 3/4 cup (full fat, <u>NOT</u> low fat) Half & Half

1 tbsp unsalted butter

1 tsp additional butter

Pinch of baking soda

Tiny dash of nutmeg (preferably freshly ground)

1 tsp vanilla extract

2 cups pecans

Small cup of cold water

2 tbsp Half & Half (set aside)

One capful (REAL, not imitation) Vanilla Extract

Servings: 12-15 pralines

Prep Time: 5 minutes
Cook Time: 45 minutes

Toast pecans in 225-degree oven for 15 minutes. Remove from oven and set aside. Lay out two rows of parchment paper near stove and workspace. Gather ingredients right next to stove where you will be making pralines. Set aside 2 tbsp half & half within your reach for tempering.

In a medium heavy-bottomed pot, add sugar, baking soda, half & half and 2 tbsp butter in that order. Turn stove burner on just past medium heat. Begin stirring and blending ingredients with a heavy wooden spoon. Continuously stir for 15-18 minutes. (Mixture will start a low, rolling boil after about 10 minutes). It should get harder to stir the longer it cooks. Drop a small bit of the mixture in the cup of water. If you can form a soft ball, stir the mixture and remove from heat. If not, continue stirring mixture for 3-4 more minutes. Remove from heat. Add pecans, nutmeg, 1 tsp butter and vanilla extract to mixture. Turn burner back on to medium and return pot to burner. Stir mixture for 5 additional minutes. If mixture seems too firm or begins to overheat before 5 minutes, remove from heat and stir in 2 tbsp half & half to thin out mixture and cool. Quickly begin dropping pralines onto parchment paper with wooden spoon. Let cool for 10 minutes.

It takes practice to perfect this technique. However, do not change the recipe or ingredients. You may learn that your stove may heat quicker or slower than mine, so you may need to slightly decrease or increase the cooking times and temperatures.

White Chocolate Apricot Bread Pudding w/ Rum Sauce

1 cup Challah bread, cubed
1 cup French bread, cubed
1 cup Boule bread or plain, white rolls, cubed
2 slices white bread, torn
1 cup dried apricots, cut into pieces
1 cup white chocolate chips
2 cups white sugar
1 cup brown sugar
5 eggs, beaten
2 egg yolks, beaten
1 cup heavy whipping cream
1 cup half & half
1 cup heavy whipping cream, divided
1/2 cup whole milk
2 tsp vanilla extract
1/2 tsp cinnamon
1/3 cup butter, softened

Servings: 12-15

Prep Time: 30 minutes
Inactive: 12 hours*
Bake Time: 1 hour

Rum sauce:
3 tbsp butter
2 cups sugar
1/8 tsp baking soda
1 1/2 cup half and half
2 tbsp Dark Rum (Brandy may be substituted)

Preheat oven to 350.

Take all bread and put in an extra-large mixing bowl. Cover bowl top loosely with wax paper or paper towel and leave in microwave overnight. *Alternatively, you may put bread in a large microwave safe bowl and microwave bread for 15 seconds; then let sit out for 20 minutes.

In an extra-large mixing bowl, cream butter and sugars together. Add beaten eggs, vanilla extract, cinnamon, milk, half & half, and ½ cup heavy whipping cream; blend well. In large bowl with breads, evenly distribute dried apricots and white chocolate chips, making sure they don't all fall to the bottom of the bowl. Pour mixture evenly over bread in bread bowl. Let soak for 15-20 minutes. Transfer contents evenly into large (5 qt) rectangular baking dish. Pour remaining ½ cup heavy whipping cream over dish. Bake in preheated oven for 50-60 minutes, checking that bread does not over-brown. Remove from oven and allow to set for 20-25 minutes.

While bread pudding is setting, begin making sauce. In a heavy bottomed pot over medium heat, add sugar, half & half, butter, and baking soda. Mix and stir well, continuing to stir until mixture starts a low boil (6-8 minutes). Continue stirring, avoiding scraping the sides of the pot and lower temperature to medium heat. Stir constantly for 10 minutes or until sauce is the consistency of a thick maple syrup. *Stir in rum or brandy. *May substitute with 1 tsp vanilla extract for those needing to avoid alcohol. Pour over bread pudding upon serving.

Pecan Praline Cheesecake

16 oz plain cream cheese

1/3 cup ricotta cheese

2 tbsp sour cream

1 tsp salted butter, melted

1 cup sugar + 2 tbsp sugar

1 tsp vanilla extract

2 eggs

1, 9 oz graham cracker crust

Servings: 8-10

Prep Time: 20 minutes
Inactive: 3 hours
Bake Time:110 minutes

Praline topping:

2 cups white sugar

1 3/4 cup Half & Half

1 tbsp butter

1 tsp additional butter

Pinch of baking soda

1 tsp vanilla extract

2 cups pecans

Small cup of cold water

3 tbsp Half & Half (set aside)

One capful (REAL, not imitation) Vanilla Extract

Heavy bottomed medium pot

Make cheesecake first. Praline topping should be made after cheesecake has set (a **minimum** of <u>3 hours</u>).

Preheat oven to 325

In a bowl, beat cream cheese, ricotta cheese, sour cream, vanilla, and sugar on high with electric mixer. Continue until all ingredients are well blended, about 3 minutes. Add eggs and continue until blended into mixture, about 1 minute.. Pour mixture into graham cracker crust. Bake 40-42 minutes (do not allow cake to brown). Remove from oven and allow to cool for 30 minutes. Refrigerate a minimum of 3 hours to overnight.

Continued on next page…

Pecan Praline Cheesecake
...continued

Toast pecans in 225-degree oven for 15 minutes. Remove from oven and set aside.

In a medium heavy bottomed pot, add sugar, baking soda, half & half and 2 tbsp butter in that order. Turn stove burner on just past medium heat. Begin stirring and blending ingredients with a heavy wooden spoon. Continuously stir for 12-15 minutes. (Mixture will start a low, rolling boil after about 10 minutes). Remove from heat. Add pecans, 1 tsp butter and vanilla extract to mixture. Turn burner back on to medium and return pot to burner. Stir mixture for 3 additional minutes.   Mixture should be the consistency of a thick cake batter (unlike when making pralines). If it seems too thick, add 1-2 tsp heavy cream. Allow mixture to cool slightly for a few minutes.

Remove cheesecake from refrigerator and slowly pour praline topping over cheesecake. Return cheesecake to refrigerator for at least 30 minutes before serving.

Pecan Pie

1 1/2 cup pecan halves; coarsely broken

1 unbaked deep-dish pie shell

1 cup sugar

2 tbsp brown sugar

1 cup light corn syrup

1/2 cup dark corn syrup

4 eggs, lightly beaten & refrigerated until ready to use

1/4 cup unsalted butter, melted

2 tsp vanilla extract

Servings: 10-12

Prep Time: 20 minutes
Bake Time: 1 hour

Preheat oven to 350.

Prepare pie shell for filling according to package directions.

In a pan over medium-high heat, add sugars and corn syrups and bring to a boil. Stir to mix well and continue stirring for 6-8 minutes. Set aside and cool for 10 minutes. In a mixing bowl, add beaten eggs, then slowly stir in sugar and corn syrup mixture; continuously stirring. Smooth mixture as much as possible. Add in butter, vanilla, and pecans. Mix well. Pour filling mixture into prepared pie shell and bake in preheated oven for 50-60 minutes or until set. Allow to cool completely before serving. This pie is great alone, with vanilla ice cream, or topped with whipping cream.

Couche Couche
(also commonly spelled Cush Cush)

1 cup yellow cornmeal

3 tbsp all purpose flour

1 tsp baking powder

3 tsp sugar

1 tbsp butter

1/2 tsp salt

2/3 cup water

1/4 cup milk

1/4 cup vegetable oil

Servings: 4

Prep Time: 5 minutes
Cook Time: 25 minutes

In a heavy bottomed pot, preferably a cast iron pot, (with available lid), heat vegetable oil over medium heat. In a mixing bowl, sift cornmeal, flour, baking powder, salt, and sugar together; blend well. Slowly stir 2/3 cup water into cornmeal mixture; mixing well. Add cornmeal mixture to heated oil, stir, and cover. [Note: During cooking time, do not attempt to break up small or medium lumps of cornmeal mixture. Bigger lumps may be broken into smaller ones]. Cook for 5 minutes. Stir, then re-cover to continue cooking for 10-12 minutes, stirring frequently. Add milk and butter to mixture and continue cooking for 2 minutes. End texture should have some random small lumps, some of which may be a bit browned. The texture should be like a slightly crumbled up muffin.

Couche Couche is one of my favorite childhood treats. It is best served hot; eaten like a cereal with milk and a dab of Steen's syrup or sugar. You can also eat it with your favorite jam.

Index:

Index:

I hope that you've enjoyed learning about my personal experience growing up in Louisiana while exploring the connection between food and culture in Cajun Country.

Now, it's time to fa do-do (go to sleep). Love & Light, *Gigi* ♥

Made in the USA
Middletown, DE
25 October 2021